LAKE FOREST LIBRARY
360 E. Deerpath
Lake Forest, IL 60045
(847) 234-0636

The Irish Civil War

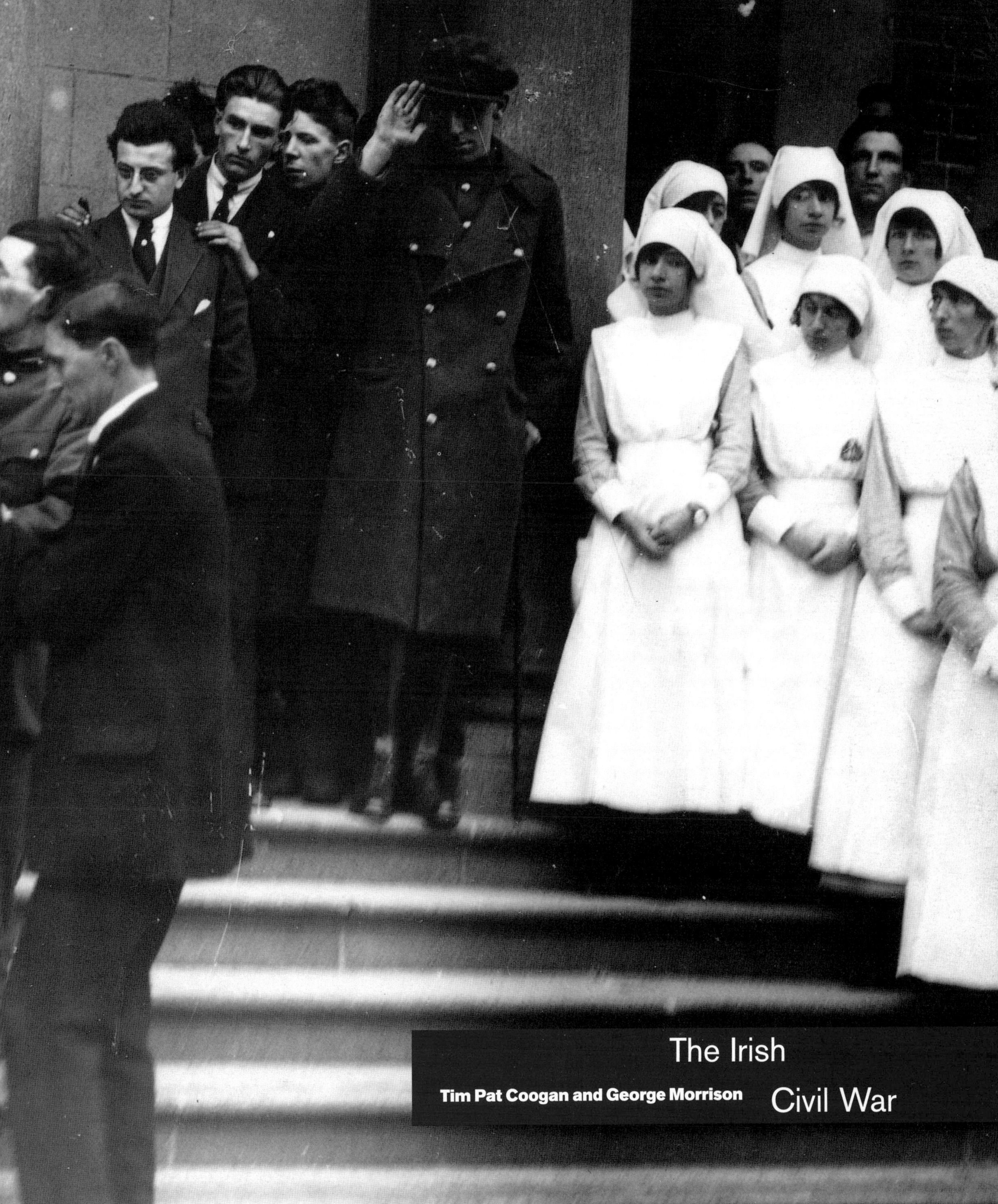

The Irish Civil War

Tim Pat Coogan and George Morrison

ROBERTS RINEHART PUBLISHERS
Boulder, Colorado

Contents

Right Liam Lynch, Commandant General of the First Southern Division of the IRA and Republican Chief-of-Staff during the Civil War.
Previous page The funeral of Michael Collins, who was killed near the end of the Civil War.

Part I

In many ways the Irish Civil War was one of the most superfluous and wasteful conflicts experienced by man since the war between the Big Enders and the Little Enders that Dean Swift described in *Gulliver's Travels* which was fought over which end of an egg should be topped at breakfast.

Normally, when viewing history, one tries to learn how to interpret contemporary events by reference to the past. By coincidence, it happened that as this book on the Irish Civil War was being prepared, the British and the Irish made a significant effort to resolve the differences between them, and those between the Orange and Green traditions, with the Good Friday Peace Agreement of Easter 1998. It was the most important accord in Anglo-Irish relations since the Treaty of 1921 which had contributed so much to the outbreak of the Civil War. A few months after its signing, in July, the Good Friday Agreement withstood the onslaught of its Green and Orange opponents during two major crises which occurred in July and August. In the first, the Orange element made a concerted effort to gain, by the tactics of petrol bomb and barricade, what they had failed to achieve at the ballot box, where the Accord was ratified by a majority of 71 per cent in favour with 29 per cent opposed. A new civil war almost broke out on the ostensible issue of upholding Protestant rights to march through a Catholic district, down the Garvaghy Road, near the town of Portadown. But the British government held its nerve and the forces of moderation, including those of moderate Protestantism, made their feelings clear in the wave of revulsion that followed the death of three small boys, the Quinn brothers, in a petrol bomb attack.

In the second, and worst atrocity, a shared approach between Dublin and London met the challenge of introducing coordinated legislation, north and south of the Irish border, to cope with the far worse carnage caused by a Republican splinter group opposed to the Agreement, which set off a bomb that killed more children. The explosion this time

A Republican soldier, wounded in the 1922 siege of the Four Courts, Dublin, is helped to an ambulance by a Free State soldier.

The Irish Civil War

Its origins and course

claimed 28 lives, and inflicted horrific injuries on scores of innocent civilians, both Catholic and Protestant, in the predominantly Nationalist town of Omagh.

Thus it was possible to contrast how the concerted efforts of the British and Irish leaders, Tony Blair and Bertie Ahern, to find agreement bore fruit on these occasions, compared with what happened in the twenties. During the modern negotiations, aid from the Americans, along with the presence of a former Finnish prime minister and a former chief of staff of the Canadian Army, assisted the delegates through various bad patches. Not only was none of this outside influence available when the earlier treaty was brokered, the principal Irish leader, Eamon de Valera, stayed away from the talks and deliberately set out to create divisions within the delegation which he sent to negotiate in his stead with the flower of Imperial England. Anything positive which de Valera achieved constitutionally in the years that followed the sanguinary conflict could have been achieved without a shot being fired. However, illogicality is no barrier to deep feeling, and the divisions which the Civil War highlighted have lasted to this day. Partition is still in place and the two big political parties of southern Ireland, Fianna Fail and Fine Gael trace their origins to that tragic split.

The Civil War, like bankruptcy, came in two ways: gradually and suddenly. The gradual way had its roots in the Home Rule controversy which had convulsed Irish political life for almost a century beforehand. We will return to the sudden way later. Home Rule, the grail towards which Irish Nationalists strove, had been voted on several times before the Treaty occurred. There was no dispute about the fact, that from 1886 onwards when Gladstone first espoused the Home Rule cause, in successive elections the sentiment of the population overall remained that recorded in 1886, which was roughly 86 MPs returned for Home Rule with only 17 opposed.

Irish Nationalist affection for Home Rule was not based on any abstract, sentimental ideal. From the time union with the rest of Britain was imposed in 1800, there were several practical reasons for the Irish wishing to break the union. It differed markedly from the relationships that bound Scotland and Wales to Westminster – Ireland was forbidden the right to trade directly with the colonies, thus fostering stagnation in its economy. The Act further denatured the natural commercial, artistic and political life of Dublin by transferring not only the seat of government to London but everything that went with it: patronage, high society and artistic life as well as important commercial and administrative organizations. In these circumstances, absentee landlords, the fall in agricultural prices and the population explosion that had followed the end of the Napoleonic Wars all contributed to the mismanagement of the Irish land system that helped to create the great famine of the 1840s.

In the north, however, where the Loyalist and Protestant population enjoyed a more favourable system of land tenure, heavy industry took root, thereby creating Protestant wealth and sectarian strife, as Catholics tried to compete for jobs. A certain ethnic factor added to the bitterness of relationships because many of the Protestant population were the descendants of Scots settlers who had been given land in the 'plantations' of earlier centuries during which the native Catholic Irish were dispossessed. Towards the end of the nineteenth century Belfast grew into a red-bricked Mancunian industrial city. Around it were the neatly tended farms of the north-east which in appearance had more in common with the Scottish lowlands than the lush, unkempt fertility of the south and south-west of the country. The visual differences which met the eye were replicated in the politics of the day.

As Nationalist and Catholic support for Home Rule grew, a pithy phrase was coined which explains why six of Ireland's north-eastern counties are still part of the United Kingdom today. Randolph Churchill declared on behalf of the Tories and Unionists that 'Ulster will fight and Ulster will be right'.[1] The alliance between Tory England and Unionist Ireland encapsulated in that Churchillian phrase was one which combined at other crucial junctures in Irish history to interact with domestic British politics in a manner which was to have serious consequences in Ireland.

The involvement of the Irish issue with the Corn Laws controversy, which convulsed the Tory Party, brought down Sir Robert Peel's government in 1846 and helped to spread famine in Ireland during the 1840s. A further such juncture in our day delayed the kind of agreement arrived at on Good Friday 1998 until the arrival of a Labour majority at Westminister independent of Unionist support. Previously, because of the Tory divisions over Europe and a small Tory majority, the Unionists were able to utilize their strategic position in the House of Commons to delay talks by demanding that the decommissioning of IRA weapons be made a pre-condition for commencing negotiations.

Randolph Churchill was, of course, moved by concern for the Tories rather than the Unionists. As he told a friend, 'I had decided some time ago that if the GOM went for Home Rule, the Orange card would be the one to play. Please God it may turn out the ace of trumps and not the two'.[2] It was an ace for the Tories. Backed by the Conservatives, the Irish Unionists, particularly those in north-eastern Ireland, successfully resisted the introduction of Home Rule for which the majority of the Irish electorate had overwhelmingly voted. In the ensuing political turmoil, Gladstone fell and although the Nationalists continued Parnell's technique of using the Irish Parliamentary Party at Westminister to play off one of the great British political parties against the other, the Tory-Unionist alliance continued to frustrate the will of the ballot box.

However, in the years of what is known to history as 'the Ulster crisis', prior to the outbreak of World War I, the Irish Parliamentary Party managed to bring the Home Rule issue back to a point where once more Home Rule appeared to be on the verge of enactment. The House of Lords veto was removed so that once the Bill passed three readings it could not be prevented from becoming law. But once more the Tories and the Unionists combined to 'play the Orange card'. The two main players were the leader of the Unionists, Edward Carson and Bonar Law, who led the Conservative party. Carson was a Dublin-born Protestant lawyer of Scottish descent who found favour in British eyes by becoming a zealous crown prosecutor. From this role, Carson spring-boarded into becoming a Unionist MP for Trinity College, Dublin, one of the top earners at the English Bar and a member of the British Wartime Coalition Cabinet. Carson personified the 'crown prosecutor' mentality of traditional Unionism's core philosophy: Nationalism and Home Rule were a treasonable product of Vatican-conditioned rebel minds which could only be countered by means that went beyond the parliamentary arena.

Apart from the politics of the situation, Bonar Law empathized with the Carsonites. He was a clergyman's son of Scots Presbyterian descent who had spent a great deal of time in Ulster. But the overriding motor force of the Tory policy at the time was the political one. There are two sides to politics, an inside and an outside. The Tories had been outside for a long time and were not too particular about how the 'Orange card' was played, provided it once again turned out to be an 'ace of trumps' for them. Their attitude was summed up by British Conservative Party leader Bonar Law in 1912 during a speech in Belfast at what was described in the press as 'the wedding of Protestant Ulster with the Conservative and Unionist Party'. It was to prove a blood wedding. Bonar Law threw down the gauntlet against the Home Rule proposals, which looked like coming to fruition under the Liberal government led by Herbert Asquith, using imagery based on the Siege of Derry:

Fianna na h'Éireann boys wait on Howth Pier on 26 July 1914, to help unload the arms on board the *Asgard*, brought in by Erskine Childers, seen here in oilskins on the extreme right of the photograph.

Once more you hold the pass, the pass for the Empire. You are a besieged city. The timid have left you; your Lundys have betrayed you; but you have closed your gate. The Government have erected by their parliamentary act a boom against you to shut you off from the help of the British people. You will burst that boom. The help will come and when the crisis is over, men will say to you in words not unlike those used by Pitt – you have saved yourself by your exertions, you will save the Empire by your example.

The word 'example' in Bonar Law's harangue was significant. Groups of Irish Nationalists began to think that they, too, should take a leaf out of the Conservative and Orangemen's book of defiance. Secretly, a group of Irish Republican Brotherhood (IRB) leaders began to plot armed rebellion. Publicly, constitutionalists like Professor Eoin MacNeill of the National University, unaware of the IRB men's secret intentions, began to organize as the Orangemen had done, but with the opposite intention – to create an Irish National Volunteer corps to ensure that Home Rule would be carried into law should the will of Parliament be defied by armed Orange rebels. Such resistance to Home Rule became increasingly likely after Bonar Law followed up his wedding oratory a couple of months later with another speech, this time at Blenheim Palace on 24 July 1912 at which he said:

We regard the government as a revolutionary committee which has seized upon despotic power by fraud. In opposition to them we shall not be guided by the considerations or bound by their restraints which would influence us in an ordinary constitutional struggle... I can imagine no length of resistance to which Ulster can go in which I should not be prepared to support them, and which, in my belief, they would not be supported by the overwhelming majority of the British people.

To add point to his remarks, the Ulster Volunteer Force (UVF) openly ran in 300 tons of rifles to Ulster from Germany, while the British Army stood idly by during these proceedings. The officers commanding the Curragh in County Kildare, effectively the British Army's nerve centre in Ireland, had made it known that they would not proceed against the Ulstermen if ordered to enforce Home Rule against their wishes. Instead of being court-martialled for mutiny, the Irish General Officer Commanding, General Gough, returned to Dublin from London in triumph. He bore with him a document drafted by the Orangemen's chief supporter at the War Office, General Sir Henry Wilson, authorizing himself and his officers to flout the will of Parliament. By way of underlining the depth of resistance, hundreds of thousands of Ulster Protestants, led by Carson, signed a covenant, some apparently in their own blood, promising to oppose Home Rule.

Above An interesting example of a rather naive British recruiting propaganda poster of 1915.
Left The Right Honourable John Redmond MP, Leader of the Irish Parliamentary (Home Rule) Party, speaking at the Kilkenny by-election, 1917.

These proceedings heightened the perception in Nationalist Ireland that although Ulster could fight and Ulster would be right, Nationalist Ireland could be as democratic as it wished but would never get its wishes granted through the ballot box.

The IRB, who by now were in effective control of the Irish Volunteers, also arranged for gun-runnings, at Howth in County Dublin and at Kilcoole in County Wicklow. Some public sympathy acrued to the Volunteers because during the Howth affair the British Army took a very different stance from the one they had held in the Ulster gun-running affair, and fired on a Dublin crowd, killing some demonstrators. But whatever the IRB leadership planned, there was still no general intention of turning the Howth-Wicklow weapons either on the British or on the Orangemen. In fact, when the Great War broke out in 1914, a sizeable proportion of the Nationalist Volunteers followed the lead of the Irish Parliamentary Party leader, John Redmond, and enlisted in the British Army to fight for the rights of small nations. A smaller section, however, decided that the war offered an opportunity to strike for freedom while England was preoccupied.

The 1916 Rebellion was the result. The rebels seized a number of strong points in Dublin and held them for a week until they were blasted out of their positions by an overwhelming superiority in numbers and the use of heavy artillery. Initially, the rebels were highly unpopular for two reasons: the destruction caused by the fighting did not win them much support amongst the populace; and a great many Irish families had relations fighting in France. The rebel prisoners were booed as they were marched to the docks en route to British prisons. However, the subsequent executions of the Rebellion's leaders swung the pendulum of support away from the government to the Volunteers. People began contrasting the executions policy and the fact that the Army had shot Dublin demonstrators, with the leniency displayed towards the treasonable behaviour of the plotters in the higher echelons of the British Army, the Conservative Party and the Unionists. Why should the Volunteers not go to the same 'length of resistance to which Ulster can go' became a burning question.

Sinn Fein had almost nothing to do with the 1916 Rebellion but because the British and the media continuously referred to the 1916 Rising as the Sinn Fein Rebellion, the insurgents became known as Sinn Feiners. Ironically, Michael Collins, the principal IRB man to survive the 1916 Rebellion, was continuously at odds with the leaders of the party because he regarded it as being too moderate, although he used Sinn Fein for his own ends.

Above Two women amid the debris in the portico of the burnt-out General Post Office, Dublin, headquarters of the Republican forces in the Easter Rising of 1916. This photograph would appear to have been taken towards the end of the first week of May.

Left Surrendered Republican forces of the 1916 Rising being marched through the streets of Dublin under prisoners' escort in May of that year.

The 1916 insurgents had declared a republic and this general aspiration appeared to be seconded by the very large poll secured by Sinn Fein in the 'Khaki' election which followed the ending of the war in 1918. Sinn Fein obliterated the Irish Parliamentary Party and recorded the same sort of result which had been accorded to supporters of Home Rule at successive elections held since 1886. Sinn Fein won 73 out of a total of 105 seats, swamping the Irish Parliamentary party which won only six, a loss of 74 seats. The Unionists won the rest. Their poll of 315,394 votes out of a total of 1,526,910 votes indicates how much support the Unionists might have looked to in support of their defiance had they not been supported by the Conservatives.

Sinn Fein had stood in support of an all-Ireland republic, whose representatives would sit not at Westminister, but in Dublin. However, appearances were deceptive. Much of the Sinn Fein support came from a public not so much affirming its desire for war as recording a thank you for peace. After the 1916 Rising, Sinn Fein had mobilized the popular antagonism towards the idea of enforced conscription in Ireland to such a pitch that the idea had to be abandoned. However, backed by its mandate at the polls, Sinn Fein reaffirmed the declaration of the Republic first proclaimed in 1916, at a meeting of the Dail (Parliament) in January of 1919. Sinn Fein's military wing, the Irish Volunteers, which became known as the Irish Republican Army (IRA) from this Dail sitting, now began to go to war. The British had created a favourable climate for IRA operations by banning the Dail and arresting most of the newly elected Sinn Fein deputies, including Eamon de Valera. Michael Collins, however, escaped and began pioneering a new type of urban guerrilla warfare, which ensured, that unlike 1916 confrontation, the insurgents would not waste their time seizing buildings from which they could easily be removed by superior fire-power. It was a war characterized by ambushes, reprisal and counter-reprisal. The Irish could not hope to defeat the British by conventional means but they scored notable propaganda triumphs through a combination of skilful publicity and Collins's unique talent for securing and making use of intelligence.

Restrained by public opinion from putting forth its full military strength in Ireland, the British cabinet, a coalition of Liberals and Conservatives led by Lloyd George, were forced to adopt the concept of a 'police war'. The idea was that the British were engaged in putting down, not a war of independence, but a criminal conspiracy, with the aid of special 'police'. These included two distinct groups: the Auxilliary Cadets, ex-British officers who were paid 10 shillings a day, and like the IRA, used unorthodox methods and elected their own officers; and the more numerous Black and Tans. These were

Above Ireland's first Sinn Fein banner. Eamon de Valera, the sole surviving leader of the 1916 Rising, was elected a Dail Deputy (Republican National Assembly) for the Sinn Fein Party on 11 July 1917. The Bailieboro branch of the Sinn Fein Party decided to name their branch after de Valera.

Left Irish Republican Army men on the march in 1920.

ex-servicemen who were given a free hand to make Ireland 'an appropriate hell'[3] for rebels. They earned the nickname 'Black and Tans', culled from a famous pack of fox hounds, from their khaki jackets and black trousers. In effect, it was a war between two secret services.

The Irish assassination of British spies and policemen, combined with a skilful use of publicity, eventually forced the British to the conference table in 1921. Prior to the outbreak of the Great War, the British had been preparing a solution to the Irish issue based on partition. Although the idea was neither widely popular nor greatly discussed openly, there was a growing belief in the minds of some decision makers that Ireland should be divided. The predominantly Catholic south and south-western counties would go to the Catholics and Nationalists, and the nine predominantly Protestant counties comprising the northern province of Ulster would be Unionist. Partition was not welcome to either the Nationalists or the Unionists. The Nationalists wanted Home Rule for all Ireland and the Unionists wanted it for none, wishing instead that Ireland remain under the crown.

A point which is often overlooked by Republicans, and indeed, by Tories and Unionists, is the fact that the more enlightened British government opinion at the time believed that it would be in the best long-time interests, both of Ireland and England, to have a united Ireland. The more far-seeing imperialists of the day, like Lord Birkenhead, realized that a peaceful, united Ireland offered better prospects for both Ireland and England than a divided and turbulent one. In fact Birkenhead once admonished the Unionist leader, Lord Londonderry, for his provincialism, stating bluntly that: 'the admitted circumstances that if the political considerations allowed it, the economic and financial interests of Ireland would be greatly benefited by union, however long postponed'.[4] But postponed it was, and still is.

The Irish Committee on Ireland recommended to the cabinet on 17 February 1919 that: 'The whole of the province of Ulster should be included in the Northern Parliament. The Committee consider that a Northern Parliament consisting of the nine counties in Ulster is more likely to lead to the ultimate union of the whole of Ireland than if the Northern Parliament was composed of six counties only'. A cabinet meeting held in Downing Street at the end of that year (on 3 December) confirmed that view, saying that: 'the general feeling was that the ultimate aim of the Government's policy in Ireland was a united Ireland with a Parliament of its own'.[5] However, this was not the Unionists' viewpoint and they used their leverage to see that their will prevailed.

Above British Prime Minister David Lloyd George and behind him, the Chief Secretary for Ireland, Sir Hamar Greenwood, review a contingent of Black and Tans in London during March 1920, as they are about to be sent to Ireland.
Left A platoon of motorized Black and Tans outside Harcourt railway station in Dublin in April of the same year.

On 15 December 1919 the cabinet was informed that the Unionists were worried about their ability 'to govern Northern Ireland where there was a Nationalist majority, and greatly preferred that the scheme should be limited only to the six Protestant counties'. Nevertheless, at the next cabinet meeting (on 19 December) it was still 'strongly urged' from the British side that the new state should include the whole of Ulster. But the Unionists had a powerful ally in the ranks of the British cabinet in the form of Arthur Balfour. It was Balfour, who, as Chief Secretary for Ireland had been Carson's mentor, becoming known in the process as 'Bloody Balfour'. He backed the Unionists' arguments. The 'six Protestant counties' were accordingly decided on, even though these counties had Catholic majorities in Fermanagh and Tyrone and the city of Derry. The 19 December meeting acknowledged that: 'The jurisdiction of the Northern Parliament over the whole of Ulster as a geographical unit was more logical and in many ways easier to defend in Parliament...'. Nevertheless it 'was generally felt that it was *even more important* to get a scheme, even though theoretically less perfect, that would meet with general acceptance'.

An argument which swayed the British at the time was proposed by Sir James Craig, who had succeeded the aging Carson as the Unionist leader; he put forward the proposal that a Boundary Commission be set up to establish the wishes of the populations on either side of the border. The idea was that the Commission would ascertain whether the populations wished to be included in the six counties or in the new Irish Free State which was envisaged for the South. But, as events would prove, the British were merely attracted to this idea, not wedded to it. The fundamental aim of their policy was to get the troublesome Irish issue off the British cabinet agenda once and for all. Accordingly, the British began to administer the partition prescription in 1920 by passing the Government of Ireland Act, which provided for a parliament and a six-county statelet made up of six of Ireland's north-eastern counties. The Act also provided for elections to be held on 21 May 1921. At these elections Sinn Fein triumphed even more conclusively than before, winning 124 seats unopposed. In the north, where the elections were characterized by ferocious violence, personation and gerrymandering, the Unionists won 40 seats. When the king opened the new parliament in the following month, Lloyd George had arranged for the monarch's speech to include conciliatory remarks written for him by the South African leader Jan Smuts, amongst sentiments of a more menacing character provided by Arthur Balfour. The King's delivery of Smuts' text provided an opportunity for the Nationalists to grasp the olive branch and declare a truce which came into effect on 11 July 1921

Above A Royal Irish Constabulary Auxilliary and two Black and Tans beside a Crossley tender protected by chicken-wire against hand grenades. This photograph was taken during the summer of 1920. These vehicles, thus protected, were known as 'chicken coops' and led the IRA to develop grenades with hooks.
Left A mixed group of RIC Auxilliaries (with leather gaiters) and Black and Tans (wearing puttees), in Ireland during the summer of 1920.

Incredible though it seems now, neither the mass of the IRA nor of Sinn Fein appears to have grasped the fact that by then Ireland was effectively partitioned. Of course, de Valera and Collins knew very well what was happening. Not only was partition a *fait accompli*, a republic for the rest of Ireland was also out of the question because of the British Imperial mindset of the time. What was done in Dublin could set a precedent for other parts of the British Empire – Cairo and New Delhi, for example.

It is important to bear in mind that from 11 July until 6 December 1921, the Irish engaged in a negotiation concerning the type of state which would be acceptable to the British within a predetermined area: the remaining 26 counties which comprise today's Irish Republic. The actual Treaty negotiations were conducted between an English delegation and a Southern Irish one. Although the Dubliners were naturally resentful of Partition and argued strongly against it during the talks, there were no Unionists present. Sir James Craig had his six counties and his only concern, as the Dublin and London delegations battled it out, was to ensure that Belfast continued to remain untouched by their disputation. His influence was exerted, via the Conservatives, through figures like Balfour. Accordingly, both the negotiations and the subsequent Dail debates, had a certain Alice in Wonderland quality about them.

This pall over the negotiations was both heightened and obscured by the rivalry between Eamon de Valera and Michael Collins, the two most powerful and charismatic figures on the Irish scene. The two men were as different as Danton and Robespierre. Collins was the youngest of a large family, doted on as a child and raised by a loving mother and equally devoted elder sisters. De Valera was the illegitimate son of Catherine Coll, a maid-servant who had emigrated to New York from County Limerick . She rejected the child and sent him to be reared by his uncle in Ireland. Their differing backgrounds showed in the personalities of the two men: Collins was boisterous, exuberant and outgoing, with an unholy habit of indulging in impromptu wrestling matches in which the prize or forfeit was a 'piece of ear' – the winner biting the ear of the unfortunate victim. That sort of behaviour would have been unthinkable to the remote, austere de Valera who taught mathematics and studied Machiavelli.

The other less obvious, but highly significant source of tension between them was the origins of their power. De Valera was the elected president of Sinn Fein, the last surviving leader of the 1916 Rebellion, who had escaped the firing squads by a hair's breath because revulsion against the executions policy had enforced leniency on the British

At a meeting in the Mansion House, Dublin, on 18 May 1922, the pro-Treaty and anti-Treaty politicians signed a pact relating to the forthcoming general election; after the meeting this photograph was taken in the garden of the Mansion House.

government. An obvious source of Collins's influence was the manner in which he reorganized the revolutionary movement after 1916 while de Valera was either in jail or in America, and the rest of the Sinn Fein leadership was in jail. But there was another force behind Collins – the secret Irish Republican Brotherhood, the IRB. The IRB elected Collins as its president shortly after de Valera had been smuggled aboard a liner bound for America as a stowaway, by Collins, who had earlier sprung him from jail. Thus, according to the constitution of this powerful body, which played such a vital role in the affairs of Ireland from before World War I until the ending of the Civil War in 1923, Collins was not only the president of the IRB, but also the real president of the Irish Republic.

The Civil War cannot simply be explained in terms of the conflict between Collins and de Valera, but it can be said with certainty that the effect of de Valera's break with Collins in the perfervid and complex situation which prevailed at the time of the truce, was many times more damaging than if say, in our time, the Sinn Fein leader, Gerry Adams, turned on his colleague, Martin McGuinness over the terms of the contemporary Peace Agreement. The result was that the divisions and strands of dissent, which were bound to emerge over any such agreement, acquired a powerful and charismatic leader in the shape of de Valera, which in turn gave the forces of opposition a strength they would otherwise not have had.

While in America de Valera achieved some valuable publicity for the Irish cause in the US but he also provoked damaging splits in the ranks of Irish Americans in a manner which foreshadowed his subsequent conduct in Ireland. By the time he slipped back in to Ireland at Christmas 1920, again as a stowaway, the truce was only a little over six months away. Meanwhile, Collins, who had been almost unknown when de Valera left for the States in mid-1919, had been tranformed into an international hero, the Irish de Wet. He had doggedly endured a daily regime of near escapes and back-breaking work. Although there was a price on his head and he knew that capture meant torture and death, Collins organized a successful national loan in which everyone got their receipt, as well as continuing to cycle around Dublin openly, seeing his contacts, collecting information, arranging arms supplies and prosecuting the war.

The President of Sinn Fein, Eamon de Valera, addressing a large audience in the United States during his stay there in 1919.

Nevertheless, practically the first thing de Valera did on returning to Dublin was to attempt to get Collins out of the country to America, ostensibly to carry on publicity work. Collins refused to go, telling friends: 'The long whore won't get rid of me that easily'.[6] But when the truce came, de Valera refused to include Collins in the delegation which he brought with him to London to commence negotiation with the British. He gave as his reason for this snub the fact that he did not wish the British to have the opportunity of taking pictures of Collins, who hitherto had avoided British attention because they did not know what he looked like. Of course, had Collins gone to America, as de Valera wished, the British could have had him photographed to their hearts' content.

In London de Valera left his delegation in a hotel while he conducted a series of *tête-à-tête* meetings with Lloyd George. The two men spent several hours together alone. Between them they probably possessed the shrewdest political minds in the Europe of their day. There is no possibility that de Valera did not have the most minute grasp of what was on offer: an acceptance of Partition; an Irish Free State with the same Dominion status as Canada or Australia; an oath of allegiance to the Crown; and the installation of a governor-general. Ireland would not have a navy, but would have its own civil service, army, police force, parliament and national flag. These were tremendous gains but they fell far short of the 32-county Republic declared in 1916 which was sanctified both by the blood of the executed 1916 leaders and the tortures, death and destruction inflicted and endured during the ensuing years.

De Valera returned to Dublin and determined to stay there when the substantive negotiations began on the British offer. Skirmishings on the nature of the British offer continued throughout the summer in a correspondence which was made public,[7] between de Valera and Lloyd George. But Lloyd George made it abundantly clear that the British would not enter negotiations on the basis that Ireland was 'an independent and sovereign state'. That, said the British prime minister, was an 'impossible' basis for negotiation. A republic was out of the question. He told de Valera in a letter dated 18 September 1920, that: 'From the very outset of our conversation I told you that we looked to Ireland to own allegiance to the Throne, and to make her future as a member of the British Commonwealth. That was the basis of our proposals, and we cannot alter it. The status which you now claim for your delegates is, in effect, a repudiation of that basis.'

Later in the month on 29 September, Lloyd George brushed off another attempt by de Valera to slip into the negotiations without preconditions by stating in writing that: 'The position taken up by His Majesty's Government is fundamental to the existence of the British Empire and they cannot alter it.' However, in the same letter he again issued an invitation to 'a conference in London, on 11 October, where we can meet your delegates as spokesmen of the people whom you represent with a view to ascertaining how the association of Ireland with the community of nations known as the British Empire may best be reconciled with Irish national aspirations'.

Obviously the Unionists were not amongst the people whom de Valera represented, but he accepted the invitation the next day. Furthermore, his letter of acceptance reiterated Lloyd George's wording above, that the proposed conference would be held 'with a view to ascertaining how the association of Ireland with the community of nations known as the British Empire may best be reconciled with Irish national aspirations'.

Robert Barton, one of the Irish negotiators who signed the Treaty but later joined de Valera in rejecting it, said of these preliminaries: '...the English refused to recognize us as acting on behalf of the Irish Republic and the fact that we agreed to negotiate at all on any basis was possibly the primary cause of our down fall. Certainly it was the first milestone on the road to disaster'.[8] Collins, who backed the Treaty, judged that: 'if we all stood on the recognition of the Irish Republic as a prelude to any conference we could very easily have said so, and there would have been no conference...it was the acceptance of the invitation that formed the compromise'.[9] Though he never admitted the fact in so many words, de Valera thought so too. Two remarks of his, made while he was selecting the delegation to go to London, sum up his position. He referred to the need to get out of 'the strait jacket of the Republic'[10] and stated that, 'we must have scapegoats'.[11] The principal scapegoat was to be Michael Collins. For de Valera now proceeded to abandon his arguments about photographic opportunities and used his enormous psychological force to brow-beat Collins into going to London while he stayed at home.

Collins, more than any man alive, understood that once a truce came, the Irish had lost their most valuable weapon, secrecy. Not only was he identifiable, so were his network of agents and principal henchmen. Once a truce came he said the IRA would be 'like rabbits coming out of a hole'.[12] However, while being very conscious of his military weakness, he was equally clear that the opportunity of setting up an Irish free state, with or without capital letters, was too important to miss. There had been other lost opportunities before in Ireland's past which had cost her Home Rule, the fall of Parnell in 1890, among them.

Accordingly, after much heart-searching, he agreed to engage in a fore-doomed struggle to harmonize the aspirations of the men of 1916 with the realities of Imperial politics in London. Another member of the delegation who went with him to London was

Arthur Griffith, the founder of Sinn Fein who was also a brilliant journalist. However, he was in his fities and was badly affected by imprisonment and years of overwork. Other delegates included: Eamon Duggan and Charles Gavan Duffy, both solicitors; Robert Barton, a landowner, and his cousin Erskine Childers, the author of the *Riddle of the Sands*. Childers had successfully sailed from Germany with the guns landed for the Nationalists at Howth, pre-1916. Childers was the official secretary to the delegation and Griffith was the nominal leader, but because of his health he asked Collins to lead. He had agreed to go only out of a sense of duty and told de Valera that 'I know and you know that I can't bring back a Republic'.[13]

De Valera would later write that he had deliberately built divisions into the delegation. He said he had not chosen either Cathal Brugha or Austin Stack because the former would have created wasteful rows, and Collins and Griffith would not work with Stack.[14] Brugha was a fanatical Republican who would settle for nothing less than the Thirty-two County Republic declared in 1916, and politically and personally was completely hostile to Collins. Stack, too, was opposed to Collins whose mercurial energy and lack of respect for demarcation lines, led him to intervene frequently on turf which Stack, as the Sinn Fein Minister for Home Affairs, considered belonged to him. Collins had further rubbed salt into Stack's wounds by making public references to his inefficiency. In the divided Sinn Fein cabinet, de Valera had taken care to side with both Brugha and Stack. He also took steps to ensure that their brand of Republicanism was represented in London. He expected that Collins and Griffith would accept the Crown, but that Childers, an 'intellectual Republican', and Barton would counterbalance them. Duffy and Duggan, he said, were mere padding. To send such a delegation to London, while he stayed in Dublin, was obviously creating the conditions for a split.

But de Valera would later argue that a formula of his invention, External Association, would have bridged the gap between Crown and Republic. The idea was that Ireland would become an external associate of the British Commonwealth if recognized as an independent Irish State by both Great Britain and the Commonwealth. He had thought better of presenting this proposal to Lloyd George after meeting him in July, but now, in October, he gave it to the Irish plenipotentiaries as the basis of an unfinished Draft Treaty A. He also furnished them with an equally unfinished Draft Treaty B which contained the terms of a settlement which the Irish were to use for propaganda purposes if the negotiations broke down. But what these terms were, exactly, was not spelt out. De Valera merely wrote to Griffith saying: 'We must depend on your side for the initiative after this'.[15]

A look at this lack of back-up and the divisions to which the Irish delegation were deliberately subjected, helps to illuminate the reason why this account of the origins and course of the Civil War began by contrasting the scene-setting for the Anglo-Irish negotiation of 1921 with those of 1998. In 1922, no supportive phone calls came from the White House as the Irish were confronted by one of the most powerful delegations that Imperial England ever brought together. Winston Churchill only ranked fourth on the team, which was led by Lloyd George, the 'Welsh Wizard' who had also led the 'Kitchen Cabinet' which defeated Germany. He was supported by the leader of the Conservative party, Austin Chamberlain, a committed Unionist and son of Joseph Chamberlain, the opponent of Home Rule who did much to bring down Parnell. The third of the big four on the British side, Lord Birkenhead, the Lord Chancellor, was also closely associated with the Unionist cause. As F.E. Smith, he had acted as a galloper for Bonar Law at his great Balmoral Rally, becoming known as 'Galloper' Smith as a result. These men were supported by a number of other political colleagues and by the resources of England's brilliant Imperial Civil Service.

But not only did de Valera undercut his delegation in London; part of his manoeuverings at this time included an attempt in Dublin, in Collins's absence, to gain control of the Irish army. The army was rapidly expanded during the truce, greatly exceeding the numbers of the original IRA, which still formed its core, both in membership and leadership. De Valera was checkmated by Collins's IRB supporters amongst the leadership. One leader, Ginger O'Connell, summed up the mood by saying there was no need for a reorganization (involving the issuing of new commissions, placing Stack in a position of authority in GHQ and the taking of a new oath which would effectively have given de Valera control) by saying: 'We are a band of brothers'.[16] De Valera did not react to this opposition with a display of brotherly love. Rising excitedly, he pushed away the table in front of him and, half screaming, half shouting, said: 'Ye may mutiny if you like, but Ireland will give me another army' and dismissed the meeting.[17] When he calmed down, however, de Valera realized there was no possibility of Ireland giving him another army and he dropped his proposals.

Suffice it to say, that against this backdrop, several weeks of tortuous negotiations ensued in London during which Collins constantly visited Dublin, and de Valera was kept informed of what was happening, but still refused to go to London, though repeatedly asked to do so. The following assessment of their position drawn up by Collins and Griffith sums up their attitude in London to the pressures bearing upon them and indicates how they came to sign the Treaty:[18]

Collins *How best to reconcile our ideas with the fixed ideas at present held by certain members of the cabinet? I will not agree to anything which threatens to plunge the people of Ireland into a war – not without their authority. Still less do I agree to being dictated to by those not embroiled in these negotiations...if they are not in agreement with the steps we are taking, and hope to take, why then do they themselves not consider their own presence here in London? Example: Brugha refused to be a member of the delegation.*
Griffith *It is not so much a question of who is dictating to whom. It is a question of powers invested in us as representatives of our country. Sooner or later a decision will have to be made.*
Collins *Exactly. What are our powers? Are we to commit our country one way or the other, yet without authority to do so? The advantages of Dominion status to us as a* stepping stone *(author's emphasis) to complete independence are immeasurable.*
Griffith *Agreed, but with one question. How far can we trust the signatures of the British delegation in this matter? Once signed we are committed. But are they?*
Collins *No, we are not committed – not until both the Dail and Westminster ratify whatever agreement is made.*
Griffith *Ratification by the Dail means what precisely? That a certain amount of power is still in the hands of those we know will be against anything which treats of Empire status.*
Collins *I agree in part to the above. Supposing, however, we were to go back to Dublin tomorrow with a document which gave us a republic. Would such a document find favour with everyone? I doubt it.*
Griffith *So do I. But sooner or later a decision will have to be made and we shall have to make it – whatever our position and authority.*

The decision to accept Dominion status for 26 of Ireland's partitioned counties was made at around 2.30 am on the morning of 6 December 1921. Publicly, Collins would defend the Treaty on the grounds that while it did not extend full freedom to Ireland, it did provide a stepping stone to, as he put it, 'freedom to achieve freedom'.[19] Privately, as we shall see, he attempted to use the stepping stone as a jumping-off point for securing control of the partitioned six counties by military means. Knowing how his Conservative and Unionist supporters would view the measure of independence which was being conferred on the Irish, Birkenhead turned to Collins after the signing and said: 'I may have signed my political death warrant'. Collins replied: 'I may have signed my actual death warrant'.[20] He had.

De Valera later argued and had the fact inscribed in his official biography, that he had not known of the Treaty signing until he saw the evening papers. He said that he had heard of a treaty being signed and was ready to throw his hat in the air, thinking that a republic had been achieved and partition avoided, but that he was horrified when he learned what had really been accepted. These are completely untruthful statements.[21] In fact, shortly after the signing, the news was telephoned from London to the O'Mara home in Limerick where de Valera was spending the night. However, he refused to go to the phone when invited to do so by Richard Mulcahy who took the call. De Valera and Brugha travelled up to Dublin on a train later in the day, sitting apart from Mulcahy and others who, like them, had been attending a function in Limerick. These seating arrangements led to an oft repeated comment: 'The Civil War was organized on that train.'[22]

The day after the signing of the Treaty, de Valera called a cabinet meeting of the Sinn Fein ministers still in Dublin and announced that he intended asking for the resignations of the signatories. To his amazement he was opposed by William T. Cosgrave whom he had hitherto regarded as the most docile member of the cabinet. Cosgrave argued that Griffith, Collins and Barton should be heard before being sacked. Accordingly, as Cosgrave's vote would have made it four-three against de Valera, Brugha and Stack, de Valera shelved the sacking proposal. Instead he issued a public statement saying that 'In view of the proposed Treaty with Great Britain, President de Valera has sent an urgent summons to the members of the Cabinet in London to report at once so that a full Cabinet decision may be taken. The hour of the meeting is fixed for 12 noon tomorrow, Thursday. A meeting of the Dail will be summoned later.'[23]

This was the first open step towards civil war. After an acrimonious cabinet debate in which de Valera objected principally to the fact that the delegates had not referred back to him before signing, nor achieved external association, a vote was taken in which Cosgrave sided with the delegates. After the vote de Valera was appealed to by several members of the cabinet not to oppose the decision publicly because of the dire consequences which would follow. However, he proceeded to take another major step towards civil war by issuing the following press statement:

The terms of this agreement are in violent conflict with the wishes of the majority of this nation, as expressed freely in successive elections during the past three years. I feel it my duty to inform you immediately that I cannot recommend the acceptance of this treaty either to Dail Éireann or to the country. In this attitude I am supported by the Ministers of Home Affairs and Defence... The greatest test of our people has come. Let us face it worthily without bitterness, and above all, without recrimination. There is a definite constitutional way of resolving our political differences – let us not depart from it, and let the conduct of the Cabinet in this matter be an example to the whole nation.

De Valera then revealed to Erskine Childers what he meant by a 'definite constitutional way'. He intended to adopt a policy of attracting 'extremist support'. Childers noted in his diary that de Valera's 'nerve and confidence are amazing, seems certain of winning. Will put up a scheme productive of real peace'.[24] However, de Valera's subsequent behaviour was to prove neither productive, peaceful, nor an 'example to the whole nation'. In the Treaty debate in the Dail, he continued to follow the line he'd adopted in the private cabinet altercations, that the worst aspect of the Treaty was the manner in which it had been signed, i.e., without consulting him. He described himself as a captain of his ship whose crew had let him down, to which Collins replied 'A Captain who sent his crew to sea, and tried to direct operations from dry land'.[25] The record of the debate shows that he contributed almost twice the amount of verbage of Collins and Griffith combined: a total of 39 pages for him to 20 for them.

Inside the chamber he made a total of 250 interruptions, using his prestige to overrule procedures while outside the chamber he attempted again to take control of the army and sought to influence individual deputies by calling them in and haranguing them. De Valera principally rested his case on a reworking of his External Associations proposal, which the delegates had put to the British in London, but which had been rejected two days before the Treaty was signed. This reworking became known as Document No. 2. It recognized partition, but managed to avoid referring either to an oath or a republic. It did concede that 'for the purpose of the Association, Ireland shall recognize his Britannic Majesty as head of the Association'.[26] In the end even de Valera realized that this document was going nowhere and withdrew it after Griffith had released it to the press.

Various initiatives aimed at bridging the gap between Document No. 2 and the Treaty were tried and failed. Collins accepted a Labour Party formula whereby it was proposed that the Dail would pass legislation enabling a provisional government to be formed as a committee of the Dail. This government would then draw up a constitution which would derive its authority not from the Crown but from the Irish people. Thus the oath could be sworn to, even by Republicans, because they would be swearing allegiance to an Irish Free State constitution. However, de Valera rejected both this compromise and a further initiative based on it.[27]

A group of pro- and anti-Treaty deputies was mobilized by Sean T. O' Kelly whereby it was 'respectfully' suggested that de Valera 'might advise abstention from voting against the Treaty'. The deputies advised this course in the hope that it would preserve 'the services of President de Valera' for the nation. It was intended that he would continue as President of the Dail but that 'the provisional government would be permitted to function by the Dail, and derive its powers from the Dail'. Thus the Dail would continue to control the army and other services. Again Collins and Griffith accepted the compromise. Again de Valera rejected it. The war of words spread outside the chamber. By now the sparks generated in Dail debate were beginning to fall on pools of petrol spilled throughout the country. Outside the arena of the Collins-de Valera rivalry, or the shared antipathies of Brugha and Stack, there was a genuine widespread Republican opposition to the Treaty. The oath, the imposition of a governor-general, and of course, partition, were anathema to many. Another factor which was to come into play was the disorganized nature of the conflict which had just ended. Local IRA commanders were far more influential than faraway figures in Dublin. IRA volunteers went pro- or anti-Treaty, depending on the political colouration of their Officers Commanding.

Brothers were to die fighting on opposite sides. Families would be sundered for generations over the cataclysm which was to befall Ireland. People had joined the revolutionary movement for all sorts of reasons. Some because of an act of brutality on the part of the Crown forces. Some for socialistic reasons, to alleviate the appalling poverty of the slums, or to break up big farms and distribute land to the landless. Some had merely acted out of a general impulse towards freedom motivated by Ireland's history: the butcheries inflicted by the yeomanry during the 1798 Rebellion; the horrors of the Famine; the subsequent battle against landlordism which had led to the shootings, burnings and animal mutilations of the land war. Others out of a sense of outrage at the Conservative-sponsored defiance of democratic procedure by the Protestants of north-eastern Ulster.

After the truce there was a prevailing sense in the IRA and for a time, amongst the public, akin to that of the British 'brass hat' generals of World War I: 'One good push and we'll win the war'. Many a hot-blooded young IRA volunteer believed that having come this far, another round would gain the Republic. Some simply felt that to sign would be a betrayal of all they had fought for. They had never expected to defeat the British Empire, but fought simply to keep alive the 1916 Rising tradition of having 'a rising in every generation', no matter how hopeless.

The following popular ballad of the time sums up the feeling of many a young IRA man:

But why should words my frenzy whet
Unless we are to strike
Our despot lords who fear no threat
But reverence the pike
Oh, do be wise, leave moral force
The strength of thought and pen
And all the value of discourse
To lily-livered men.

Against this emotionalism and idealism, three principal factors weighed with the Collins faction. One, the IRA simply did not have the ability to restart the war, to fight by conventional methods and to drive the British from Ireland's shores. Two, the continuation of guerrilla war was now impossible; and three, the majority of the people wanted peace and, like Collins himself, did not want to let slip the measure of freedom now on offer.

The Dail debate is remarkable for the amount of verbiage bestowed on the symbolic aspects of the Treaty, the oath and the governor-general, in contrast with the amount of time devoted to discussing the substantive issue of partition. Only a tiny handful of the delegates even referred to the North. The *fait accompli* of partition was understood, but not stated. The more one studies the Dail proceedings of the day, the more appropriate Swift's Big Ender and Little Ender analogy becomes.

In a sense, these proceedings represented a certain coming home to roost of chickens which Collins himself had loosed. With de Valera and most of the other political leaders of Sinn Fein in jail, he and his close associate, Harry Boland, had manipulated the list of candidates which Sinn Fein had put up for election in 1918, so that only men of 'forward' views were selected. People inclined to seek compromise or preach that dreaded doctrine 'moderation' were firmly eschewed. Both Boland and Collins were destined to fall in the Civil War. Nevertheless, in the course of the debate, a combination of IRB manipulation and much impassioned oratory, some of which actually articulated the obvious wishes of the mass of the electorate, finally resulted in acceptance of the Treaty. The crucial vote, on 7 January, was 64 to 57 in favour.

De Valera greeted the result by leading his followers out of the Dail in protest, thereby depriving the new State of its democratic opposition at birth. When he led them back in again it was purely for obstructive purposes. It has to be remembered that these were very simple days, pre-television and before the widespread introduction of education . A true story illustrates how de Valera could get away with his behaviour over the Treaty while still retaining respect. It concerns an election in Clare during which de Valera stopped his car to ask an old man whom he saw sitting on a ditch, for his vote. As he approached, the old man asked him was he 'one of those political gentlemen from Dublin?' De Valera opined that he was, whereupon the old man took his pipe out of his mouth, spat and said: 'Ye's are wasting your time. Down here, we're all up for de Valera'.[28]

Having been ratified by the Dail, the Treaty provisions required that it be subsequently ratified both in the House of Commons and the House of Lords in London, and that a new constitution be prepared and an election held in Ireland. These official steps commenced immediately after the Dail passed the Treaty. In England, Churchill shepherded the Treaty through the Commons in the teeth of a howling gale of Tory and Unionist opposition. Birkenhead did likewise in the House of Lords. Thus both men, despite their Imperialist backgrounds, have some claim to the paternity of today's Irish Republic.

Republicans of the period, however, were far from accepting of any such legitimizing process. As Collins set up his constitutional committee to draft the new Irish constitution, and liaised with the British on matters such as the handing over of barracks and other strategic buildings, including Dublin Castle, anti-Treaty fervour spread its alchemy through the country. IRA units divided and those who took the anti-Treaty position began raiding for arms and money, as the Provisional government, headed by Griffith and Collins, shut off payment to anti-Treaty army units. In the early post-Treaty debate days these units probably represented a majority of the IRA. Within three days of the Treaty being passed, IRA officers met in Dublin and declared that: 'The action of the majority in the Dail in supporting the Treaty involving the setting up of an Irish Free State was a subversion of the Republic and relieved the Army from its allegiance to An Dail'.[29]

Above The handover of the Bank of Ireland to Free State authorities in March 1922; Commissioner Barrett and Captain Haylett shake hands.
Left Free State Guard taking over the British Army barracks at Parkside Street, Dublin, in 1922.

This meeting ultimately led to the setting up of an Army Executive which repudiated the Dail's authority. After it forced the holding of an Army Convention against the Provisional government's wishes on 26 March 1922, the Executive men, led by Rory O'Connor, were formally cut off from government funding or support. The handover of barracks from British to Irish hands meant that some barracks and equipment went to Executive supporters. Local loyalties meant that in parts of the country, particularly Cork, Kerry, Mayo, Tipperary and Sligo, anti-Treaty forces held sway. A majority of the people wanted the Treaty. They had given Sinn Fein a vote as a reward for peace in the first place, not a blank cheque for war, but apart from a cohort of people around Collins in Dublin, not very many people were articulating the peace viewpoint. A famous quotation from the pro-Treatyite minister Kevin O'Higgins, who, like Michael Collins, was destined ultimately to be gunned down by Republicans, summed up the new government's position as consisting of: 'Simply eight young men in the City hall standing amidst the ruins of one administration, with the foundations not yet laid, and with wild men screaming through the keyhole. No police force was functioning through the country, no system of justice was operating, the wheels of administration hung idle, battered out of recognition by the clash of rival jurisdictions.'[30]

It was both an accurate and yet unfair description. Accurate insofar as it articulated the difficulties experienced by the architects of the new State, but some of the Treaty's opponents were not 'wild men', in the sense of being mere thugs or bank robbers. Even though thuggery and robbery did follow from their actions, the Executive leaders were, in the main, men of integrity and principle. Liam Lynch of Cork was such a figure, even though he fought to the bitter end and beyond it. So too, were other leaders such as Rory O'Connor and Ernie O'Malley. O'Malley, although a diehard amongst diehards, was a Republican chronicler of great literary skill, whose unpublished diaries are a treasure trove for historians and whose published works are a chilling must for anyone interested in Irish history. His self-sacrificing character may be deduced from a letter he wrote while on a 40-day hunger strike. He had been in very bad physical shape before the strike began, through a combination of the hardships of the Black and Tan War and was so badly shot up in the Civil War that sixteen bullets had to be removed from his body. Nevertheless he wrote, even after the Civil War had ended months earlier in calamity for his side: 'I hope the men will last: I am afraid some are rather weak, but so long as even a few stick it to the end it will save the situation…the country has not had, as yet, sufficient voluntary sacrifice and suffering, and not until suffering fructuates will she get back her real soul.'[31]

That is the authentic voice of intransigent Republican martyrdom, but it is so far from the language of politicians charged with administering the mundane affairs of men, that one can readily see how, despite the seeming strength of the IRA, once the fighting began, a majority of the electorate would decide that it had had more than enough 'voluntary sacrifice' and opt for the Treaty.

Before the all-out shooting war began, the anti-Treatyite takeover of strongholds resulted in some notable flashpoints. At Limerick, for example, it appeared that Arthur Griffith was driving into a death trap when he went to address a pro-Treaty rally despite the fact that the city had been taken over by the anti-Treatyites. He made his will and left a letter to his friends to be opened in the event of his death, urging them to stand by the Treaty; but in the event his courageous action paid off. The speech was safely delivered and fighting avoided. Collins had similar brushes with death. Revolvers were fired in crowds as he spoke at public meetings, railway tracks were torn up to prevent people coming to hear him, and on one occasion a train from which he attempted to address a crowd, was driven off while he was in mid-sentence.

Bank robberies, raids on post offices and levies – to uphold the Republic, their authors claimed; to support thirsts, those who had to pay them averred – continued to be the order of the day. Although the situation was highly combustible, the basic disinclination of Collins to turn Free State guns on his former colleagues and a reciprocal feeling on the part of many of his prominent adversaries, prevented the outbreak of general warfare. However, it became increasingly clear that hostilities could not long be avoided after the seizure of the Irish legal system's nerve centre, the Four Courts in Dublin, by the 'irregulars' as the pro-Treatyites increasingly dubbed their opponents, on 13 April 1922. The Four Courts were taken as part of a general seizure of strong points in Dublin, including haunts of the *ancien regime*, like the Kildare Street Club and a number of Masonic halls, which gave the commandeerings a sectarian patina. The seizures thus worried the British and the former Unionists still living in the South, and vastly confirmed Unionist fears in Northern Ireland, an area where the situation was so complex and so bloody, that events there will be treated separately (*see page 38*).

It would be true to say that in the period from the passing of the Treaty in January until the middle of June 1922, that the principal motor forces in Irish affairs were military ones. But that did not prevent de Valera from trying to assert his authority by getting control of the political steering wheel through attracting 'extremist support'. A series of speeches which he made in March 1922 remain an irradicable blot on his long and distinguished career. At Dungarvan on 16 March he said: 'The Treaty…barred the way to independence with the blood of fellow Irishmen. It was only by Civil War after this that they would get their independence…if you don't fight today, you will have to fight tomorrow; and I say, when you are in a good fighting position, then fight on'.[32] From Dungarvan he headed further into Republican heartland, to Carrick-on-Suir in County Tipperary, where his intention would appear to have been to celebrate St Patrick's Day by wetting the Shamrock with blood. Speaking to a crowd which is generally estimated to have included at least 700 IRA men, he said:

If the Treaty was accepted, the fight for freedom would still go on; and the Irish people, instead of fighting foreign soldiers, would have to fight the Irish soldiers of an Irish government set up by Irish men. If the Treaty was not rejected, perhaps it was over the bodies of the young men he saw around him that day that the fight for Irish freedom may be sought.

Later that day at Thurles, again speaking to a predominantly IRA audience, in which many of his listeners were carrying rifles, he said much the same and added that 'they would have to wade through, perhaps, the blood of some of the members of their Government in order to get Irish freedom'. The following day he spoke in Killarney, County Kerry, which would later see some of the most tragic and bloody events of the entire Civil War. The *Irish Independent*'s report of his Kerry utterances (20 March) contained the following: 'Acts had been performed in the name of the Republic which would be immoral if the Republic didn't exist…Men and women were shot for helping the enemy, and there would be no justification for the shooting of these if the Republic did not exist'. He declared that if they accepted the Treaty, they were putting two very definite barriers in the way of achieving freedom. One barrier, according to de Valera, would be that they were pledging the nation's honour to a certain agreement. The other barrier, if an Irish Government was set up, would be that those who wanted to travel on the road to achieve freedom, such as those men present with the rifles, would have in the future not merely the foreign soldiers to meet, but would have to meet the force of their own brothers, their fellow countrymen, who would be supporting the government.

'Therefore in future', he went on, 'in order to achieve freedom, if our Volunteers continue, and I hope they will continue until the goal is reached, if we continue on that movement which was begun when the Volunteers were started, and we suppose this Treaty is

De Valera surrounded by a cordon of men holding hands in order to protect him after his release from prison.

ratified by your votes, then these men, in order to achieve freedom, will have, I said yesterday, to march over the dead bodies of their own brothers. They will have to wade through Irish blood...The people had never a right to do wrong'. He was certain that the same pluck which had carried them so far would enable them to finish.

Many years afterwards when de Valera had become a revered icon amongst his fellow countrymen, not least because he had outlived most of his contemporaries, he published his authorized biography which said of these statements: 'There is no evidence that his speeches, in fact, stirred up the violence they were said to encourage'.[33] This is an ingenious piece of sophistry because short of leaving placards on dead bodies saying 'shot because of de Valera's speeches', there is no way one could produce such evidence. But at the time his wild and whirling words produced such a storm of criticism that he attempted a defence in a letter to the *Irish Independent* (on 23 March) in which he said that his speeches were only 'an answer to those who said the London Agreements gave us "freedom to achieve freedom"'. He said that attempts to characterize his utterances as incitements to Civil War were 'villainous'. But there can be no ambiguity about 'an Easter Proclamation', as he termed it, which he issued after the Four Courts seizure:

Young men and young women of Ireland, hold steadily on. Those who with cries of woe and lamentation would now involve you in a disastrous rout you will soon see rally behind you and vie with you for first place in the vanguard. Beyond all telling is the destiny God has in mind for Ireland the fair, the peerless one. You are the artificers of that destiny. Yours is the faith that moves mountains, the faith that confounds misgivings. Yours is the faith and love that begot the enterprise of 1916. Young men and women of Ireland, the goal is at last in sight – steady, all together forward. Ireland is yours for the taking. Take it.

While de Valera protested that these speeches had no bearing on the Civil War, and that he viewed events as 'through a glass darkly',[34] such policy statements coming from a man of his eminence, the senior survivor of 'the enterprise of 1916', obviously had to have an effect on the general public. His espousal of 'extremist support' in his battle with Collins had placed him in the position of having to use the classic excuse of the demagogue: 'There go my people. I am their leader. I must follow them'. O'Connor, O'Malley and their associates, did not consult de Valera about the Four Courts' seizure. In fact, O'Connor had previously given a press conference at which he stated that while de Valera was the political leader whom he and his colleagues most admired, nevertheless, he said in answer to a question, a reporter was free to describe the type of government which he proposed to set up as 'a military dictatorship'.[35] He said he had not read Document No. 2 and did not understand the Treaty.

The day after the seizure, a Labour Party delegation met de Valera to plead with him to use his influence with the Four Courts men to avert disaster. They pointed out that the majority of the people had voted for the Treaty. De Valera's response was to state at least a dozen times that 'The majority have no right to do wrong'.[36]

Ernie O'Malley has left a vivid account of how he and O' Connor spent the afternoon of the Four Courts seizure.[37] They had afternoon tea and played classical music. As Schumann's *Carnival* died away O'Connor said: 'We must go down town now'. The carnival stopped on 28 June 1922. Collins was finally driven to act against the Four Courts men by a combination of circumstances. Firstly, the Four Courts garrison was an ever-growing threat to the Provisional government's authority. The Executive not only directed robberies and holdups, but did everything it could to frustrate the Provisional government's attempts to form either an army or a police force.

Collins tried to overlook these obstructions for the sake of unity by concluding a highly dubious electoral pact with de Valera. This envisaged both sides putting forward a panel of candidates under the banner of Sinn Fein on the basis of their Dail strengths from which subsequently a cabinet would be elected, including 'Extern Ministers' who would be members of government but would not have to take the hated oath. Thus de Valera, Brugha, Childers and Stack could all have entered government while still repudiating the Treaty. The details of the pact appalled Collins's cabinet colleagues when they became known. Relations between himself and Griffith never regained their former cordiality in the short time left to both men.

Collins had four reasons for agreeing to the pact. The first was for British consumption; he explained that despite the growing state of anarchy in the country, the pact made it possible to hold the election called for by the Treaty. A second reason was that the pact postponed the evil hour of confrontation with his former friends in which he might conceivably have created a constitution which would somehow square the circle between British Imperial requirements and Rory O'Conner's Republican aspirations. A third reason was that the pact bought time to build up and train an army and police force.

Fourthly, delay enabled Collins to continue with a breathtakingly illegal undercover piece of co-operation with the Four Courts' leadership. Without official sanction, and possibly even without the knowledge of a majority of his cabinet colleagues, he prosecuted an undercover, cross-border war in support of the Catholics who were under a state of bloody siege in the Six County state. The forces directed against the Catholics were mobilized and trained by Field Marshall Sir Henry Wilson, with the direct approval and support of the Northern Ireland prime minister, Sir James Craig. Craig said of Wilson, 'He is my only guide as to what steps are necessary. Everyone else is brushed aside. All suggestions will be put before the Field Marshal and if he recommends them I'll carry them out.'[38]

In a very real sense Collins was fatally to agree with this assessment of Wilson's importance. His four-pronged policy fell apart in June. Firstly, his hopes for the constitution were dashed. Collins had directed his draftsmen to produce a document which clearly derived its authority solely from the Irish people. It contained no reference to either an oath or a governor-general, both sicking points for the British government. Churchill described Collins's proposed document as being 'of Bolshevic character' and Lloyd George called it a 'complete negation and complete evasion of the Treaty'.[39] Of all the fraught meetings which took place at Downing Street between Irish and British leaders during this period, those arising from the Free State constitution were to prove the most acrimonious and difficult.

After reading the document Churchill told Collins that his government: 'had made one surrender after another to the Republicans and had not obtained the free opinion of the Irish people' thereby causing himself and the other British signatories of the Treaty to be 'subjected to a fierce scrutiny of our actions' from right-wing Tories and their Unionist allies. He told Collins: 'You will find that we are just as tenacious on essential points – the Crown, the British Commonwealth, no Republic – as de Valera and Rory O'Connor – and we intend to fight for our points'. At another juncture Collins lost his temper with Lloyd George and said that he would have been shot had he fallen into British hands, unlike Childers whom the British had released 'after half an hour because he was an Englishman'. Lloyd George replied coldly that they 'would indeed have shot him'. Afterwards he and the distinguished civil servant, Lionel Curtis, discussed Collins's behaviour. Lloyd George said that he was 'just a wild animal, a mustang'. When Curtis said that negotiating with Collins was like 'trying to write on water', Lloyd George commented: 'shallow and agitated water'.

Inevitably, the stronger side got the constitution it wanted. The governor-general and the oath were reintroduced and Collins allowed publication of the document to occur only on the morning of the election, when its appearance probably did very little to influence matters one way or the other. The Pact also went. After leaving Downing Street with his constitutional hopes dashed, Collins went to Cork where he delivered a widely reported speech repudiating the Pact.

The death of Sir Henry Wilson proved to be one of the final, not just straws, but tree trunks which smashed the camel's back of restraint towards the Four Courts men. Wilson was shot dead on the steps of his home in London on 22 June 1922 by two IRA men. One of them, Joseph O'Sullivan, was a one-legged man who had no hope of escaping. His companion, Reggie Dunne, stayed with him after the shooting and paid with his life for his gallantry on the scaffold with O'Sullivan a few weeks later. The assassination of Sir Henry Wilson is one of the great Irish whodunnits. Was it directed by the Four Courts men or by Collins as part of his secret northern offensive?

I believe that the answer may have been both. Reggie Dunne, who was trusted by both the Four Courts men and Collins, is known to have visited the Four Courts men and Collins before crossing to London. From my researches I am inclined to believe that having spoken to both sides, Dunne believed that shooting Wilson would provoke a reaction from the British that would have the effect of uniting both factions of the sundered IRA and cause the resumption of war with a view towards securing a 32 county Irish Republic free of partition, oaths and governor-generals. It was a doomed vision, but it almost provoked the reaction the assassins sought. For a moment the British did tremble on the verge of a resumption of hostilities. General Macready, the officer in charge of British forces in southern Ireland, was ordered to storm the Four Courts. Churchill made a statement to an enraged House of Commons in which he said:

The presence in Dublin of a band of men styling themselves the Headquarters of the Republican Executive is a gross breach and defiance of the Treaty. The time has come when it is not unfair, premature or impatient for us to make to the strengthened Irish Government and new Irish Parliament a request in express terms that this sort of thing must come to an end. If it does not come to an end, if through weakness, want of courage, or some other less creditable reason it is not brought to an end and a speedy end, then it is my duty to say, on behalf of His Majesty's Government, that we shall regard the Treaty as having been formally violated, and we shall take no steps to carry out or legalize its further stages, and that we shall resume full liberty of action in any direction that may seem right and proper, or to any extent that may be necessary to safeguard the interests and rights entrusted to our care.[40]

However, wiser councils prevailed. The British realized that far from eradicating the menace to the Treaty posed by the Four Courts occupation, they would compound it. In securing a building they would lose Irish public opinion and unite the pro- and anti-Treaty IRA. Macready's attack was delayed. Then the Four Courts men proceeded to lose pro-Treaty opinion . At this time, as part of the general campaign of hostility towards the new Six County regime, both wings of the IRA were co-operating in prosecuting a 'Belfast boycott'. This was, in effect, a trade war directed against Northern-produced goods and services. In the course of a raid on a Dublin garage to seize vehicles and petrol to help in furthering the embargo, a prominent Four Courts officer was captured.

The Four Courts men retaliated by capturing the man responsible for training the Provisional government army, General Ginger O'Connell. This, coming on top of Wilson's assassination and the other events, was the last straw. Collins borrowed a field piece from Macready and commenced shelling the Four Courts in the early morning of 28 June 1922. The Civil War had officially begun. Collins had greeted Churchill's call to end the Four Courts occupation with a defiant: 'let Churchill come over here and do his own dirty work'. But, as he knew in his heart, the dirty work inevitably fell to the Irish. By the time the Civil War ended the following May, Ireland was devastated. To a heavy death toll must be added the accompanying destruction of property and infrastructure which fell on a largely rural economy and on a people who had been devastated financially and pyschologically by the Black and Tan War. There were no EU grants or subsidies, no mini Marshall Aid plans available for reconstruction in those days. The bitterness which was engendered in a small country, of 'great hatred, little room'[41], would be difficult to overstate. A family war is always the most bitter. Even today, the two main parties, Fianna Fail and Fine Gael, owe their origins to the Civil War split; Fine Gael stemming from the Collins's side, Fianna Fail from de Valera's.

Once the actual shooting began, the balance of advantage swung noticeably towards the pro-Treaty side with the holding of the election. The election had been overshadowed by the Wilson-Four Courts shelling crises, but as the dust settled the significance of the results became apparent: de Valera's faction held 36 seats, with a loss of 22; the Collins-

Griffith group held 58 seats, with a loss of 8; the Labour Party held 17 seats and the Farmers' Party seven. These results, taken with the votes of six Independents and four Unionists meant that the pro-Treaty elements had won an emphatic majority. Henceforth there would not be a great difference in the peoples' attitudes to the depredations of a foreign army and those of native sons. The ending of the Black and Tan War was the highwater mark of countrywide support for the IRA. Once Civil War began, the population experienced the effects of the loss of homes and loved ones inflicted upon them by fellow Irishmen, who in some cases, were their neighbours.

The new Free State army was inexperienced and disorganized. Nevertheless, it soon proved more than a match for the anti-Treaty IRA in open warfare. This was in large part due to the leadership of Michael Collins and the unorthodox but effective generalship of his close friend, Emmett Dalton, who pulled off some audaciously successful seaborne landings which captured the Republican strongholds of Cork and Tralee with relative ease. In addition to these, in the space of only six weeks from the outbreak of hostilities, the Provisional government took Cahir, Cashel, Clonmel, Dundalk, Limerick, Sligo, Tipperary, Tuam, Waterford and Westport.

At this stage, the fighting was conducted along more or less conventional terms. Large parties of anti-Treaty troops occupied strongholds and were driven from them by more or less similar numbers of troops who generally had the benefit of better supplies and heavy weaponry. However, from August of 1922, ironically just three days before Michael Collins was killed, the anti-Treaty forces took a decision to resort to guerrilla warfare tactics, which resulted in the war taking a grimmer and bloodier turn.

Before going on to indicate how this phase of the war was fought, it is necessary to explain something of the most hidden and most complicated aspect of Michael Collins's many-faceted policy at this stage – his attitude to Northern Ireland. The conditions in the six north-eastern counties caused Collins to adopt totally different policies towards the two parts of the country. On the one hand, he stood for the rule of law, upholding the Treaty which included recognizing Partition. But on the other hand, he secretly did everything in his power to subvert and destroy the new state. The methods he adopted included secretly paying Northern national school teachers so as to detach them from the new educational system, obstructing co-operation between the government departments of the two governments and actively fermenting armed raids on the North, and arranging for cross-border gun-running.

One of his agents in the arms smuggling was Sean Haughey, whose son Charles, ironically, would be sacked from a later Irish cabinet, unsuccessfully prosecuted on arms charges, before becoming, like Collins, a leader of the Irish State. It is very doubtful that all of Collins's cabinet colleagues knew what he was doing. Probably those close to him, like Richard Mulcahy, the Minister for Defence, were in his confidence, as were the more senior army officers, who like him, were IRB men. But the public at large was certainly in the dark. British intelligence had a shrewd idea of what was going on. However, the British government had a considerable inducement not to make any public protests, as this would have given ammunition to the Conservative and Unionist elements who were opposed to the Treaty anyhow. Collins had a number of reasons for acting so duplicitously. Firstly, there was the human one. The Catholics in Northern Ireland were suffering severely at the hands of the Orange element. He sanctioned payments for a Belfast IRA unit because of conditions which a civil service memorandum of the time described as follows:

The Volunteers were unable to carry on their daily work... There was no organized attack of North of Ireland forces. The Volunteers in Belfast were daily, however, engaged in the riots or mob element... Orange mobs continually attacked the Catholic areas. Volunteers were almost exclusively confined to beating off these attacks. The police intervened when Volunteers pressed the attack into Orange areas, and in that way Volunteers came into contact with them.[42]

But Volunteers and the Catholic population in Northern Ireland came into contact with the police in other ways also. As a result of Sir Henry Wilson's organization of the old Royal Irish Constabulary into a new force, the Royal Ulster Constabulary (RUC), the police were viewed as a counter-insurgency force directed at the Catholics. A commission appointed by Belfast Catholics in 1922 reported: 'There is little difference between these murders and the murders carried out in various parts of Ireland by the Black & Tans, except that in nearly all cases in Belfast, the bodies are mutilated'.[43] A number of notorious police officers' names passed into the folklore of Belfast. One head constable always used the bayonet on his victims, as he considered it 'prolonged his agony' and he 'didn't believe in giving them an easy death'. A prominent police murder gang, against whom no action was ever taken, included two district inspectors, two sergeants and four policemen, all of whom were identified, after a particularly controversial murder. The police shot the Duffin brothers in their home in Clonard Gardens, using a silenced revolver. Although there were no prosecutions, the case became notorious because the killers inadvertently left a dumb witness behind them at the scene of the crime. The station dog followed the police party to the Duffins' home and the district inspector who organized the murders had to return to the house in full view the following morning to recover the animal.

Alongside the police, the Orangemen had another corps, the celebrated B-Specials, whose *modus operandi* was described by the British General Ricardo, as follows: 'The B head Constable…goes to the leading local Nationalist…He tells them that they have arms and men to patrol at nights…The Nationalist is shown a list with his name at the top and is told that "if any B-man is touched, the list will be attended to from the top." This is not an effort of the imagination, but is not an uncommon arrangement.'[44] The 'arrangement' was not confined to country districts. One of the most notorious murders of the period concerned the murders of the menfolk of the MacMahon family, who were well-known Belfast publicans. A survivor of the attack, John MacMahon, has left an account of what transpired.

About one o'clock I heard the hall door being smashed in. Five men rushed up the stairs, and ordered my brothers and myself and Edward McKinney (a barman who was also murdered) out on the landing. Four of the five men were dressed in the uniform of the RIC but from their appearance I know they are Specials, not regular RIC. One was in plain clothes. They ordered us downstairs. When we got down they lined us up in the room below, my father, my four brothers, Edward McKinney and myself, against the wall. The leader said, 'You boys say your prayers' at the same time he and the others fired volley after volley at us. I think I lay on the floor for half an hour before the ambulance came.[45]

The idea behind these atrocities was either to force a general Catholic exodus from the Six County area, cow the Catholic population into submission, and/or make people unwilling to help the IRA. But along with this policy, Collins was angered on political grounds by a number of failures on the British side to enforce agreed procedures which would have introduced some element of fair play into the administration of the Northern Statelet. One of these was proportional representation which had been agreed to under the Treaty, the other was the establishment of an upper chamber which would have had a weighting aimed at redressing Catholic grievances. However, the architects of the Orange State saw to it that bi-cameralism was not allowed to rear its ugly head in the area.

give. I now propose to call off hostilities in the North and use the political arm against Craig so long as it is of use. If that fails, the Treaty can go to hell, and we will all start again'.[57]

Collins was not destined to start again. Three weeks later both he and Arthur Griffith were dead. Griffith died of a brain haemorrhage on 12 August and was buried on the same day that Sir Henry Wilson's assassins were hanged in London. Collins was killed by a sniper's bullet in an ambush in his native West Cork on 22 August. The ambush was not arranged by de Valera, as was wrongly suggested in the Neil Jordan film, although de Valera was in the area attempting to enforce his political authority with the militarists led by Liam Lynch. But when he learned that an ambush had been laid for Collins, he attempted to have it called off. Partly this was because he believed that it would be possible to obtain a better deal from Collins in his native Cork and away from his colleagues in cabinet who harboured none of Collins's reticences about fighting former colleagues. And partly because de Valera understood clearly that Collins's friends, who held him largely responsible for the Civil War, would wreak vengeance on him if they could, should anything happen to Collins.

In the event, the ambush went ahead after de Valera had stormed out of a meeting of its planners, enraged because they would not listen to him. The ambushers had decided to call off the operation and were dismantling a mine when Collins, who had been warned that something was afoot, drove in to the little West Cork valley of Beal na Blath (the mouth of flowers), in failing light, determined to show that no-one was going to obstruct his passage in his native place. He could easily have avoided the ambush, had he not insisted on stopping and jumping out of his car, saying 'we'll fight them'.[58] He was hit by one of the last shots fired in the Civil War, by a former marksman in the British army, Sonny O'Neill. The ambush epitomized all the tragedies of the engagement. It was led by Tom Hales, a brother of Sean Hales mentioned above. Tom Hales had undergone savage torture during the Anglo-Irish war at the hands of British intelligence agents, torture which drove a companion of his insane, but it neither broke Hales, nor caused him to betray Collins. Later in the war, Sean Hales would also be shot down by a former comrade.

It has often been asserted that the death of Collins caused a grimmer note to enter the war. Because of his hesitancy in turning on his former comrades, it is asserted that he would not have gone in for the heavy-handed policy of reprisals which ultimately won the war for the government forces. Memoranda written by Collins shortly before he died make it quite clear that he had reached the end of his tether of indulgence. He had come to favour reprisals against the organizers of operations directed against Free State troops. In one he wrote 'In accordance with the precedence of all civilized countries, the prominent members of the organization which plan and execute such outrages at will, together with those personally taking part in them, be held responsible and brought to account'.[59] On 9 August, after undergoing the ordeal of a Requiem Mass in a church full of the weeping relatives of nine soldiers killed by Republicans in Kerry, he wrote to his director of intelligence concerning a group of men engaged in robberies in County Wexford: 'Any man caught looting or destroying should be shot on sight'. Even before he was killed, some of his close associates were operating a 'shoot to kill' policy every bit as deadly as anything carried out by them in the war against the British. This intensified after Collins's death and the government as a whole took an increasingly hard line with its opponents, which may be calculated as beginning with what can only be termed the judicial murder of Erskine Childers in November.

It would not be feasible to attempt a full account of all that transpired from Collins's death, although a few examples of the conduct of the war in Dublin and in Cork will give an indication of the position countrywide. Before going into such detail, it should be remembered that the war burst on an island which had already undergone tremendous convulsions. To the killings and destruction of property occasioned by the Black and Tan War, the Civil War was to add a total of some thousands of deaths. Those on the Republican side have not been accurately computed[60] because of the conditions of the time and the random nature of some of the killings. It was often hard to tell whether some of the deaths were criminal actions carried out either for motives of theft and score-settling, or genuine military action. But the pro-Treaty sides' casualties are reckoned to have been approximately 750. The uncomputed Republican losses were certainly in the region of this figure, if not considerably higher, as a total of 78 Free State sanctioned executions have to be added to the total. The damage bill was reckoned at around £50 million, a colossal sum at the time.

The Republicans developed a tactic of destroying the homes of both Free State supporters and former Unionists, which cost the nation some precious portions of its heritage in the way of libraries, furnishings, paintings and lovely old mansions. They also made a point of targeting the railways, blowing up railway lines, driving engines into

The IRA targeted communications and transportation links during the Civil War. This train at Cloughjordan, County Tipperary, surrounded by Free State soldiers, was probably derailed in February of 1922 by the IRA.

stations at full speed and blowing up bridges. One such action, personally sanctioned by de Valera, the blowing up of Mallow Bridge, had the effect of cutting off one of the main arteries linking Dublin with the south.

In the North between June 1920 and 1922 alone, 428 people were killed and several times that number seriously wounded. In this period, some 23,000 Catholics were driven from their homes in a sustained effort at 'ethnic cleansing'. In the circumstances the remarkable thing about the Irish Civil War and the sectarian war which accompanied it in Northern Ireland, is not that these self-inflicted wounds took a long time to recover from, but that the small largely agricultural nation should have recovered at all. Recovered moreover with democratic institutions intact and a system of government which proved magnaminous enough firstly to encourage de Valera and his followers back into the parliamentary arena, and later, in 1932, to hand over power peacefully to him. But these developments lie outside the scope of this book. With the death of Collins, the government, now led by W. T. Cosgrave, turned its attention to the prosecution of the war in the South. A new northern policy which had been drawn up by a cabinet sub-committee, was adopted the day after Collins was buried:

As soon as possible all military operations on the part of our supporters in or against the north-east should be brought to an end... The line to be taken now and the one logical and defencible line is a full acceptance of the Treaty. This undoubtedly means recognition of the Northern Government and implies that we should influence all those within the six counties who look to us for guidance, to acknowledge its authority and refrain from any attempt to prevent it working. [61]

Although this policy in effect copper-fastened Partition and abandoned the Catholics in Northern Ireland to the tender mercies of the Orangemen, which led to decades of conflict which are (hopefully) ending as this is being written, it did what it was intended to do. The Free State government was free to set about winning the war and establishing the new state. In this they were aided not only by the will of a majority of the people, but also by the incompetence and disorganization of their foes. Courage and idealism were plentiful, military expertise and supplies were in shorter supply. For example, after the shelling of the Four Courts began, the then powerful Dublin Brigade of the IRA, commanded by Oscar Traynor, moved in to support the Four Courts men. A number of strongholds in the centre of Dublin were seized. But these were all on the opposite side of O'Connell Street, which meant that there was no way of

Some of the child refugees from Belfast being met on their arrival in Dublin towards the end of June 1922.

tunnelling through to reach the Four Courts men. Ultimately, when the Four Courts garrison had been induced to submission, it proved a relatively simple matter for the Free State troops to blast the IRA from their city centre positions also. The Four Courts seizure itself was also a model of military incompetency. Apart from constituting a classic example of the 'static warfare' which Collins had moved away from after the failure of 1916, O'Connor and his men bungled their escape plans. They had reckoned on escaping through a sewer, but had not allowed for the fact that the tidal River Liffey could cut off their route.

An effort to relieve the beleagured IRA men from the neighbouring county of Wicklow broke down at Blessington. In Dublin the IRA believed that 'a Blessington legion' was on its way to succour them. But there was no way in which the column which had seized Blessington could break through a cordon which the government had thrown around the city. In the confusion the IRA who had taken Blessington dispersed and Blessington was easily retaken. The situation which prevailed in and around the nation's capital may be gauged from instructions issued by Oscar Traynor in the few days that he managed to hold Blessington. He sent word to his Dublin followers to: 'Let the stuff come along by the means I supply, and let the men *take the tram to Terenure* and get to me at this post on foot and unarmed. This is the only possible hope of reaching me'.[62] Traynor spoke of Tipperary men in his command who were 'very anxious to get home' and who were 'completely out of their element'. He broke his followers up into small groups and told them 'not to hold towns...to hit and get away'.[63] Subsequently most of the Dublin brigade was captured while attempting to destroy bridges in north County Dublin.

The general chaos of the situation also affected the newly formed Free State army. Accounts of the period contain a litany of complaints against the newly created force on every conceivable ground from drunkenness to brutality. Yet a shared common decency for a time prevented wide-scale bloodshed. In Limerick much to the disgust of the government in Dublin, who wanted to finish off the Republicans, not negotiate with them, the Free State commander did just that. Limerick, both because of its economic and strategic importance, was, after Dublin, probably the most important military target for both sides. However, far from going for the jugular, the Free State commander Brennan was quoted as saying 'I don't see how serious fighting can take place here, our men have nothing against the other lads'. Liam Lynch, the IRA Commander, encouraged Brennan's pacific viewpoint because he too wanted to avoid Civil War.

Free State soldiers from a Crossley tender, covered by the machine gun of a Rolls-Royce 'Whippet' armoured car, are seen here planting an incendiary device in a house in O'Connell Street occupied by Republicans. This activity took place on 5 June 1922.

He hoped that by securing a truce over Limerick that he could neutralize the powerful Free State forces in the area and move on to come to some form of agreement with the Provisional government whereby both the new constitution and the Treaty itself could be revised.

Accordingly, 'the Blessed Sacrament was produced on the table'[64] and the sides agreed not to attack each other. However, fighting inevitably broke out on 19 July. Two days later, the possession of an 18-pound gun, coupled with the same sort of confusion and disorganization which had occurred in Dublin, left Limerick in the hands of Free State forces. However, the general pacific inclination on the part of leading combatants on both sides, while it did nothing to prevent the spread of chaos, did do something to restrain bloodshed for some months.

But as the effect of Liam Lynch's decision to revert to guerrilla warfare began to take effect, peace-making went into decline. The government elected by the June election took effect from the meeting of the Dail on 5 September 1922. Henceforth, the IRA would argue that the Dail which had preceded it had never been properly dissolved and regarded the Republican survivors of that parliament as a sort of home-based government-in-exile, on whom the real legitimacy of the state devolved. To further this claim to legitimacy, the anti-Treaty side created a government of the mind on 25 October. De Valera was elected president of the Republic and chief executive of the state.[65] The further from reality de Valera's circles got, the more sonorous did their language become. The 'cabinet' formed by the new state was regarded as:

Temporarily the Supreme Executive of the Republic and the State until such time as the elected Parliament of the Republic can freely assemble, or the people being rid of external aggression are at liberty to decide freely how they are to be governed and what shall be their political relations with other countries.

Just two points need concern us about this 'Cabinet Proclamation'. One, the 'Supreme Executive of the Republic and the State' not only had no real authority over any state, it did not control the IRA, and the cabinet is best thought of as a manifestation of de Valera's desire to control the 'extremist support' which he had angled for. Secondly, it was not 'external aggression' with which the Republicans would shortly have to concern themselves, but that of their former colleagues determined to uphold the Free State against them in arms. For peace moves were now virtually at an end. A number of such initiatives could be described but one in particular may be taken as driving the last nail in the coffin of rapprochment. This occurred on 6 September 1922, between de Valera and Richard Mulcahy. By now the cabinet had decided that further peace talks were futile and the gloves must come off. However, Mulcahy, in his capacity both as leader of the army and as minister of defence, decided to see de Valera on the urgings of a well-meaning Irish-American cleric, Monsignor Ryan from San Francisco, who opened the proceedings by administering a blessing to both men.

Alas, it appears the Monsignor did not use an efficacious brand of holy water. The Monsignor had assured Mulcahy that de Valera was 'a changed man'. This assurance apparently convinced Mulcahy that he should meet de Valera, under safe conduct, at the home of the distinguished Dublin doctor Robert Farnan. However, when they met, either because the atmosphere was so tense, or de Valera, with his flair for psychological scene-stealing, attempted to utilize his considerable advantage in height over Mulcahy, the two men remained standing. Mulcahy's account of the encounter contained the following:

I took the initiative in saying that the position in Ireland was that [there] are two things to my mind that were important: 1) That somebody should be allowed to work the Treaty, and 2) that if there was to be an army in Ireland it should be subject to Parliament. Given these two things I didn't care who ruled the country as long as they were representative elected Irish men and women, and I came to a full stop. The 'changed man' still standing in front of me said: 'Some men are led by faith and some men are led by reason, but as long as there are men of faith like Rory O'Connor taking the stand that he is taking, I am a humble soldier following after them.'[66]

After the meeting, Mulcahy decided that, decoded, de Valera's utterances meant that he would continue to support practices and policies which, if persisted with, would certainly destroy the new state. He decided on a most drastic course of action: reprisal executions. Nine days after meeting de Valera, he formally submitted this proposal to the cabinet who adopted it and introduced a draconian Emergency Powers bill. Far from leading to reconciliation, the meeting in Dr Farnan's house produced a piece of legislation which made any act of war by the Republicans subject to a death penalty to be meted out by a Military Tribunal. Acts of war were deemed to include everything from being found in possession of arms, looting or destroying property. The climate for implementing this fearsome piece of legislation was worsened, or improved, depending on whether one was opposed to or supported the Free State position, by a pastoral issued by the Catholic hierarchy. It appeared in the press on 10 October and contained a broadside directed at the Republicans which contained the following:

They carry on what they call a war, but which, in the absence of any legitimate authority to justify it, is morally only a system of murder and assassination of the national forces. For it must not be forgotten that killing in an unjust war is as much murder before God as if there was no war.

The pastoral went on to tell the people that they had a duty to support 'the national Government, whatever it is'. To further that support, the church had instituted a policy of excommunications and denial of the Sacrament to Republican prisoners. The pastoral was issued during a fifteen-day amnesty period to allow Republicans to hand in their arms. Decommissioning, however, proved to have as little attraction for the IRA in 1922 as it would have 75 years later when sought by the Unionists as a pre-condition to peace talks. Military courts went into operation on 15 October. Even conceding that the situation in the country was perilous in the extreme, and that the Republicans were striking hammer blows at the Free State's prospect of survival, what followed next smacks less of court proceedings, than of judicial murder.

Erskine Childers was particularly hated by the Free State side. He was regarded as having a baneful influence on de Valera, being responsible for a lot of difficulties during the Treaty negotiations, and having initiated a good deal of the property destruction during the Civil War. He was captured in the home of his cousin, Robert Barton, and found to be in possession of a small revolver which had been given to him by Michael Collins. His fate was sealed by the military tribunal. But to prepare public opinion for his death, four rank-and-file IRA men who had been found in possession of arms were executed by firing squad on 17 November 1922. Explaining the motivation behind these first formal executions of the Civil War, Kevin O'Higgins told the Dail that the four young volunteers had been shot because 'If they took as their first case, some man who was outstandingly wicked in his activities, the unfortunate dupes throughout the country might say he was killed because he was a leader, because he was an Englishman or because he combined with others to commit raids'.[67]

Childers was duly executed by firing squad on 24 November. A man of rare nobility of character, he shook hands with each member of the firing squad and beckoned them closer for the fatal moment. On the eve of his execution, he told his twelve-year-old son, Erskine, never to do or say anything in politics which could cause bitterness. Erskine junior, a Protestant, followed his father's last instructions to such good effect that he was later elected president of Ireland. However, the bitterness of the period following his father's execution made such an outcome unthinkable at the time.

Childers's death caused Liam Lynch to abandon all ideas of peace making. He addressed a letter to the speaker of the Dail four days after Childers's death, threatening 'very drastic measures' against those who had voted for the Special Powers legislation. After the letter, government ministers lived in their offices, but for a brief period nothing further was done to terrorize the ministers. IRA officers hesitated to shoot their former comrades in cold-blooded reprisals. One prominent Free State supporter, Sean McGarry, was spotted by IRA Intelligence officers on several occasions, drinking in his favourite pub and could easily have been shot, but the commanding officer, Frank Henderson, forbade it. However, an attempt to wound, rather than kill, two pro-Treaty deputies brought down the avalanche. On 7 December, Sean Hales and Padraic O'Maille, were fired upon. O'Maille survived but Hales was killed. Early the next morning, four IRA men who had been in custody for several months, and had nothing whatever to do with Lynch's letter, were taken out and shot. One of the executed men was Rory O'Connor. The other three, Liam Mellowes, Joe McKelvey and Dick Barrett, were also prominent leaders. The men were clearly shot to make a point. They came from each of Ireland's four provinces. O'Connor was not merely the leader of the Four Courts garrison, he had been best man at the wedding of Kevin O'Higgins, one of those who authorized his execution.

O'Conner had been a particular *bête noir* of the Free Staters. His reputation was such that most of the firing squad aimed their first shots at him, setting his clothes alight. Nevertheless he appears not to have been killed outright and to have himself requested a number of pistol shots from the officer in charge of the firing squad. Richard Barrett, apparently also required a multiple *coup de grace*. The executions, insofar as they were an attempt to meet terror with terror, were successful. No further deputies were shot and the Republicans were considerably demoralized. Nevertheless, the inefficiencies of the Free State army, and the stubborn resistance of the IRA by means of guerrilla warfare proved difficult to crush, particularly in remote areas of the country. An example of the situation, in Kerry in this instance, was reported in the *Irish Times* of 27 September 1922:

Free State men stand guard.

Beyond the occupation of some of the more important towns, the national forces have been able to do very little. Enemy columns several hundred strong can move along the hills in full view and complete impunity. Vessels can reach the coast with arms and supplies for the irregulars and peaceful trading ships are frequently attacked and relieved of their cargo. A shipload of petrol was lately run into Tralee and unloaded, while a strong attack on the national troops made them powerless to interfere.

It is a remarkable fact that Kerry was not regarded as a noteworthy fighting area by the IRA's Dublin GHQ during the Black and Tan War. The Kerry IRA commander, Paddy Cahill, tended to concentrate his efforts in the Tralee-Castlegregory area, rather than operate through the county as a whole. This led the chief of staff, Richard Mulcahy to make the caustic comment that, during the Anglo-Irish war: 'Paddy took his column up Sliambh Mis and stayed there'.[68] However some lessons were obviously learned during the Anglo-Irish war. Kerry's high mountains, narrow roads and poor transport and communications were made good use of in the Civil War by the Kerry IRA. Too good, because the Civil War in Kerry was to produce atrocities which rivalled or exceeded anything that happened in the North. In fact the conduct of the Civil War in Kerry helped to further a tradition of militant Republicanism which still fuels the IRA. The fighting in Kerry was especially bitter for a number of reasons: remoteness from Dublin; the character of the Kerry people; and the fact that many of the troops engaged against the Kerry IRA came from Dublin and had no empathy with country people.

They thus came to Kerry hardened in attitude and with very little inclination to produce the Blessed Sacrament at peace tables. For their part, the people of Kerry had developed habits of independence from Dublin, either during the Black and Tan War or after it. Moreover, in Kerry, isolation allowed native Irish characteristics to develop in a particularly distinctive fashion. Anyone wanting to make a friend of an Irishman would be well advised to seek out someone from Kerry. But not if they wished to make an enemy. Kerrymen do not come equipped with a reverse gear.

At the end of September 1922, the Free State authorities were made bruisingly aware of the reality of the situation in Kerry when the town of Kenmare fell to Republicans in an attack which lasted for nine-and-a-half hours. Most of the Free State troops in the area were away on missions in other parts of the country, and a very badly planned and executed raid turned into a triumph. For example, hours were wasted tunnelling through buildings to take what was believed to be the headquarters of the Free State troops only to discover that the building (the local post office) was unoccupied. Liam Lynch later complained that six of his men were drunk during the operation and another officer commented on the fact that some of the men showed more interest in the contents of the local bank than in moving on to take other buildings. Much the same comment could have been made about the troops engaged on the Free State side. But what distinguished Kenmare in the eyes of the Free State government were two particularly nasty killings. The leader of the pro-Treaty forces, a popular local figure, Scarteen O'Connor, was shot dead in a raid on his shop. He is said to have been unarmed, but in addition to shooting him, the Republicans also killed his brother.

The Scarteen O'Connor incident and the protracted nature of the conflict, combined with factors already described, helped to poison the Kerry conflict. In March of 1923 the following litany of horrors occurred. On 6 March at Knocknagoshel five Free State troops were killed and another wounded dreadfully in a booby trap. A mine was detonated in an effort to kill a Free State officer who was alleged to have tortured Republican prisoners. Allegations of torture were frequently made against Free State officers in the Kerry area and even Free State officers complained to GHQ about some army behaviour. These complaints were certainly given credence by what happened following Knocknagoshel. Paddy Daly, the officer commanding the Free State troops, issued a statement saying that from then on, Republican prisoners would be used to clear suspect mines. The day after Knocknagoshel, nine Republican prisoners were taken from a barracks in Tralee to a mined barricade at Ballyseedy Cross at 3 am. The men were tied together and the mine was detonated.

Eight of the prisoners were blown to pieces, but incredibly one, Stephen Fuller, was hurled into a field and survived. The soldiers had prepared nine coffins in Tralee, each bearing the name of a victim, and discovered too late that the remnants of the explosion only accounted for eight victims. A distraught crowd disrupted the funerals and broke open the coffins to inspect the horrific contents. In the folklore of Ballyseedy it is stated that for weeks after the explosion, 'the crows grew fat'. But the mine reprisals continued. The day after Ballyseedy, some prisoners were lucky to escape with their lives by making a break for freedom before being sent to dismantle mines at Castlemaine. On the same day, near Killarney, there was another mine explosion which killed four prisoners, and again there was a miraculous escape. One Tadhg Coffey escaped. Five other

Republicans were not so lucky when another mine was detonated at Cahirciveen on 12 March. In the Dail, Mulcahy pointed out that 68 Free State troops had been killed up to the time of the minings and 157 injured by the particularly brutal form of warfare carried on by the Kerrymen. The fact that none of the prisoners had been found guilty of any crime had no effect on the government's attitude.

Five Republicans who had been captured in an attack on Cahirciveen which preceded the Cahirciveen mine atrocity were executed on 28 March. April was marked by a number of incidents, which culminated in the tragedy at Clashmealcon Caves at Kerry Head. A IRA column led by Timothy (Aero) Lyons was trapped in the caves during a siege which lasted several days in which two Free State soldiers were killed. The caves were cold and damp and the awful conditions of the engagement were worsened by attempts to smoke the IRA men from the caves. Some of the trapped men made a desperate attempt to escape, but were drowned in the fearsome seas smashing into the cliffs. One of those who died was Aero Lyons himself. I was once told by an old IRA man that: 'Aero's dying cries still echo at Clashmealcon'. Lyons was scaling the cliffs, some say to escape, some say to surrender when his rope broke, deliberately cut by Free State troops, it is alleged. Certainly the troops fired repeatedly at his body as it lay broken on the rocks below. The cave survivors surrendered after Lyons's death and were subsequently executed. Here is a hitherto unpublished letter written by one of the executed men, James McEnery, from Tralee jail on the eve of his execution on 25 April 1923. It is written to his brother, Father Thomas McEnery:

Dear Fr. Tom,
I am leaving you all tomorrow morning. It is very hard that I cannot see you, but some day I hope we will all meet in Heaven.
I am in the Republican Army since 1916. I fought the Tans and it is very hard that it is my own countrymen are putting me to death. I forgive all my enemies.
Look after my wife and child, who is the pride and joy of my heart, and I am asking of you one request. Don't let anyone do anything to them, bring Sunny up for the priesthood. It was a pity I did not get a chance to tell a story about that 'Siege of the Caves'. It was something awful. Say masses for me and my comrades, console the mother, it was her who was kind to me and did not forget my good wife and darling child. You will get a lock of my hair from Hannah. Cheer up now dear brother and pray for me. I am proud I am dying a soldier of the Irish Republic. Goodbye dear brother and God bless you, Jim.[69]

In such terrible circumstances did the McEnerys of Ireland come to realize that idealism was no longer enough. Clashmealcom proved to be the last major incident of the Civil War in Kerry. Apart from the hammer blows to morale caused by the executions policy, internal debate as to the wisdom of continuing the war had been growing for some months prior to the Kerry atrocities. The debate had been accelerated by the decision of a prominent Republican, Liam Deasy, Liam Lynch's second-in-command, to appeal to his comrades to lay down their arms. Deasy had already come to this decision before being captured and sentenced to death by the Free State authorities. On hearing of his death sentence he asked for a stay of execution so that he could issue an appeal aimed at forestalling any further executions. The authorities allowed him to issue a direct appeal to a number of named Republican leaders, including de Valera, on 8 February. The government accompanied publication of Deasy's letter by the offer of an amnesty to all who would comply over the ensuing ten days.

De Valera met the appeal by drafting a letter of rejection which he got Lynch to sign and issue under his name, not de Valera's own. By now, de Valera's hold on reality, and indeed that of Lynch's, was becoming extremely tenuous. Lynch believed that the war could still be won with the aid of heavy weaponry imported from the continent and by launching a major offensive in England. There was not the slightest chance of any weaponry, light or heavy, penetrating first the British blockade and then the Free State authorities' defences, to land in Republican hands. And even less possibility of commencing an English campaign. The IRA had been so reduced in strength that the once powerful London brigade could only furnish a one-legged man to accompany Reginald Dunne in the assassination of Sir Henry Wilson and no get-away car could be provided, thereby guaranteeing both men's death on the scaffold. Nevertheless, de Valera wrote to Lynch at this time, telling him that in the British campaign: 'the first blow should be concerted and big, followed quickly by a number in succession of other blows'[70] It was after this that he wrote to Edith Ellis telling her that he had been: 'condemned to view the tragedy here for the last year as through a wall of glass, powerless to intervene effectively'.[71] That 'effectively' is a good indication of the de Valera style. He, and indeed all on the IRA side, were literally powerless to act 'effectively', but none the less he was far from 'powerless' to 'intervene'. Gradually, however, the impossibility of continuing the war sank in and some leading IRA men, including Tom Barry and Tom Crofts, succeeded in arranging an army convention on 23 March 1923 in the Monavullagh Mountains in County Waterford to discuss the military situation.

That situation was assessed at the time by the authoritative military historian, Florence O'Donoghue, as follows:

...the relative strengths in the lst Southern Division area at the time were: IRA, 1,270; Free State, 9,000. In the Southern Command area, which included the counties of Cork, Kerry, Limerick, Clare, Tipperary, Kilkenny, Carlow, Wexford and about half of Galway, 6,800 IRA men were opposed by 15,000 troops. In the whole country IRA strength did not exceed 8,000 at that time, and against them the Free State authorities had built up a force of at least 38,000 combat troops. The possession of barracks, armoured cars and artillery emphasized the overwhelming Free State strength.[72]

In fact the 'over-whelming Free State strength' was demonstrated as the IRA men met. The meeting had to be adjourned a number of times because of Free State activity in the area. The meeting ended inconclusively and it was agreed that another meeting would be held on 10 April at which de Valera would report back on the chances of peace. By this stage de Valera's influence was waning considerably. In fact the first business of the convention had been to argue over whether he should be admitted, or left sitting in a kitchen. There had been bickering between himself and the IRA leadership over his attempts to exert political authority over the militarists which had led him to threaten to resign his mythical presidency. After he publicized his External Association idea again as a basis for a peace settlement he was bluntly told by representatives of the Southern Division that this was unacceptable to the IRA. Document No. 2 was as much a non-starter with the IRA as it had been with the pro-Treatyites.

At a meeting on 26 Februrary Liam Lynch stressed de Valera's subordinate position and said: 'The President...is always guided by the military situation and the decision of the Executive. The question of Document No. 2 does not arise'.[73] Writing privately to de Valera he said: 'Your publicity as to sponsoring Document No. 2 has had a very bad effect on the army and should have been avoided'.

But the reality of the military situation could not long be avoided. On 10 April, Liam Lynch was shot and fatally injured. He was succeeded by Frank Aiken, commander of the Fourth Northern Division during the Black and Tan War and a leading figure in the Collins covert war against the North. The South Armagh massacre was carried out by units under his command. Yet he had been markedly reluctant to take up arms against his former comrades, and had only been driven to hostilities through being arrested by Free

State troops. Whatever the merits or demerits of Document No. 2 as a basis for a peace settlement, Aiken was prepared to listen to de Valera about the need to think politically. He had no illusions about the IRA's ability to continue the war and from his appointment, things moved swiftly in the direction of peace.

Two documents were issued to the press on 27 April, one signed by de Valera, the other issued anonymously by Aiken announcing the suspension 'of all offensive operations' as from noon on 30 April. De Valera also initiated peace discussions through two intermediaries, Free State senators Jameson and Douglas. The Free State side used the intermediaries to tell de Valera that peace would have to be based on the principle that political issues should be settled by a majority vote; that 'a clear field' would be provided 'for Mr de Valera and his followers provided they undertook to adhere strictly to Constitutional action'.[74] Arms surrenders were to be arranged 'with as much consideration as possible for the feelings of those concerned'. De Valera, however, produced counter-proposals which were clearly unacceptable to the Free State cabinet. For example, he sought the abrogation of the oath, in other words, a rejection of the Treaty which the Free State had fought a cruel Civil War to maintain. The second proposal called for the IRA to be assigned 'at least one suitable building in each province, to be used by them as barracks and arsenals, where Republican arms shall be stored, sealed up, and defended by a specially pledged Republican guard'. After the election the arms were to be either reissued to the IRA or disposed of by whatever government was then elected. Even at that stage, with defeat staring him in the face, de Valera clearly visualized a return to government. He also visualized something else – gaining control of funds which had been subscribed for the Irish Independence Movement, while he had been fund-raising in America prior to the ending of the Black and Tan War. Another of his peace proposals suggested: 'That the funds of the Republic subscribed in the US and elsewhere, and at present sealed up by injunction, shall be made available immediately for peaceful efforts in support of the Republican cause'.[75]

Years later he did get control of these funds and they helped him to fund the *Irish Press* newspaper and the Fianna Fail Party, both of which helped carry him into power in 1932. In power, he used his position to validate Michael Collins's contention that the Treaty could be used as 'a stepping stone' to independence. The border remained, but the oath and the governor-general were eventually abolished under the terms of a new constitution which was introduced in 1937.

However, in 1923, these peace proposals of de Valera's were regarded as insolent prevarications. The Free Staters kept up a ruthless onslaught on the Republicans. Apart from arrests and shootings, executions continued, although the Republicans were clearly defeated. Cosgrave said that there would be no negotiations without a surrender of arms, and that though de Valera and his followers would get every facility for taking part in an election, there would be no tampering with the oath. He told the Dail on 10 May: 'You will find that as far as the party that has promoted disorder is concerned, they are prepared to accept peace only if they are guaranteed a lease of political life. We are not going to guarantee them a lease of political life'.

Cosgrave was firmly supported in this attitute by his cabinet. Kevin O'Higgins summed up the general attitude by saying: 'This is not going to be a draw, with a replay in the Autumn'. De Valera realized that it was time to call off the match. He arranged that Frank Aiken would issue the following ceasefire order: 'Comrades! The arms with which we have fought the enemies of our country are to be dumped. The foreign and domestic enemies of the Republic have for the moment prevailed'. And on the same day, 24 May, he issued the following proclamation over his own name:

Soldiers of the Republic, Legion of the Rearguard:
The Republic can no longer successfully be defended by your arms. Further sacrifice of life would now be vain and a continuance of the struggle in arms unwise in the national interest and prejudicial to the future of our cause. Military victory must be allowed to rest for the moment with those who have destroyed the Republic. Other means must now be sought to safeguard the nation's right. . . . You have saved the nation's honour, preserved the sacred national tradition, and kept open the road of independence. You have demonstrated in a way there is no mistaking that we are not a nation of willing bondslaves. . . . The sufferings you must now face unarmed you will bear in a manner worthy of men who were ready to give their lives for their cause. The thought that you still have to suffer for your devotion will lighten your present sorrow, and what you endure will keep you in communion with your dead comrades, who gave their lives and all those lives promised, for Ireland. May God guard every one of you and give to our country in all times of need sons who will love her as dearly and devotedly as you.

The Civil War was over. In Ballyseedy, the young crows were learning to fly.

Part II

Wars do not start suddenly though hostilities often do so. All wars, particularly modern ones, have taken years of preparation, production of *matériel*, training of personnel, building of military bases and the development of specialized communications. None of this can be achieved suddenly; consequently all wars cast long shadows before them, interpretable to those whose studies have made them able to read the signs of danger. Our Irish Civil War was no different in this and it is worthwhile spending a short time to gain a glimpse of the increasing pressures and accumulating constraints that brought about our greatest social disaster. 'War' said Clausewitz 'is the continuation of policy by other means', but never does this phrase seem more cynical and elitist than when applied to a civil war, a war in which a community is split and the two sides turn against one another. It is usual for a civil war to occur under unstable conditions, and historical developments had long prepared this situation in Ireland, even as they had done so some two and a half centuries earlier in England. The Elizabethan 'plantation' in Ireland and the Cromwellian disruption were followed by the arrival of both Scottish Covenanters and Presbyterians fleeing from their native England on account of religious persecution by supporters of the Established Church. The 1798 Rising in Ireland had had protagonists drawn from all religious denominations with the exception of the Society of Friends whose pacifist benevolence has an enduring place in Irish history. The British authorities saw in the nostalgic movement of Orangism a political device supportive of the maintenance of the Union of Ireland and Great Britain of 1801. Three more nationalist Risings took place in Ireland, in 1803, in 1848 and in 1867. In each of these the involvement of Protestants declined progressively, though less in the leadership than among the rank-and-file. None the less, in certain Protestant families a tradition of Republican separatism, derived directly from the French Revolution, maintained itself in every new generation. In 1886, influenced by the policy of Parnell and the Irish Parliamentary Party at Westminster, the British Prime Minister Gladstone, leader of the Liberal Party then in power, introduced a bill that would give Ireland a measure of Home Rule. This bill was vigorously opposed by the Conservative Party in England and by Unionists in Ireland. Gladstone's bill was defeated in the House of Commons and his government fell, to be replaced by a Conservative administration.

1. Kilmainham Gaol Doorway

The Seeds of War

Continuation of policy by other means

2

2. Lord Randolph Churchill, father of Sir Winston Churchill, was elected as a Conservative candidate for the British Parliament in 1874. When Gladstone's Liberal Party won power in 1880, Churchill formed a splinter group of Tories and Conservatives known as the Fourth Party. Vigorously opposing the Irish Home Rule Bill, he declared that 'The Orange card is the card to play', and while in Belfast, he addressed a large meeting of Unionists and Orangemen saying that, in opposing Home Rule, 'Ulster will fight and Ulster will be right!' The subsequent 'playing of the Orange card' by succeeding generations of British political opportunists was to prove one of the underlying causes of continuing instability and social unrest in Ireland.

3. A military training camp in Ireland, 1890. The closing years of the nineteenth century represented the apogee of the British Empire; so completely has this empire vanished that it is quite hard for us today, to imagine the atmosphere that prevailed in Ireland at the turn of that century. An empire must have soldiers and soldiers must be trained. The Irish barracks were filled with the troops of the military garrison, and summer camps for the training of the volunteer militias were a common sight.

4. A Protestant Sunday School procession in Parsonstown (now Birr). Imperial militarism suffused even the environment of children at this time. The Boys' Brigade, whose members may be seen at the lower left of the photograph, was a youth movement founded in 1883 that preceded Sir Baden Powell's Boy Scouts, but like it, dressed its members in the uniform of soldiers. The pill-box caps and tunics make these young boys appear like so many young Caligulas of their day.

3

4

5

6

5. The main gate of Dublin Castle, 1890. Dublin Castle was the seat of the British administration in Ireland under the Union, where the chief government official, at this time called the Lieutenant General and General Governor of Ireland (often loosely called the Viceroy) presided and held his court. Here investitures, receptions and State balls took place. On this sunny morning before the turn of the century, the gates are opened for the arrival of the Lieutenant General, coming from his official residence, the Vice-Regal Lodge in Phoenix Park. The garrison guard is lined up to await his arrival.

6. The picture gallery, Dublin Castle. No reigning British monarch had visited Dublin for almost fifty years, since Queen Victoria did so with the Prince Consort in 1851. The furnishings had become somewhat run down and seedy, and the threadbare carpets and cheap mass-produced bentwood chairs gave an air of dilapidated grandeur to the interiors, although the Audience Chamber and St Patrick's Hall were in somewhat better condition.

7. Constance Gore-Booth in her debutante's gown in the late 1890s. The social functions held at Dublin Castle were attended by those who, having been presented at Court, were eligible to receive invitations; these consisted in the main, of Unionist county families from among the Protestant, and to a lesser extent, the Catholic landed gentry, ecclesiastics, higher civil servants and a few of the more successful professional men. Among the debutantes of the late 1890s was Constance Gore-Booth and her sister from County Sligo. Here she is seen in her first court dress, an astonishingly beautiful girl, who, a little later married an impoverished Pole, Count Markievicz; the marriage was not to be a happy one. Earlier in the nineteenth century, the Gore-Booths had sponsored the emigration of many of their tenants to America. Family tradition asserted that a whole shipload of emigrees was drowned within sight of the shore. This recollection produced a profound effect on this beautiful girl, leading her to undertake social work that gradually drew her into the very midst of active political life in Ireland as a Socialist and a Nationalist.

7

8

10

9

8. Guests leaving Upper Castle Yard in a private brougham after a reception at Dublin Castle, spring 1900. As the nineteenth century drew to a close, conditions in Ireland seemed to be more stable, largely due to the Land Purchase Annuity Scheme, which was finally brought fully into operation by the Wyndham Act of 1903. This act had been introduced by the British government to assist farmers to buy their land from the landlords. As the asperities of the Land War of Parnell's time were gradually eliminated, it seemed that a political *modus vivendi* might be reached that could perhaps result in the gradual constitutional change in the status of Ireland, in accordance with the policy of the Irish Parliamentary Party at Westminster.

9. James Connolly, the great Labour leader and Commandant of the Irish Citizen Army in the 1916 Rising, is seen here with his wife and children. Connolly was born in County Monaghan in 1870 but his parents emigrated to Edinburgh soon after his birth. At the age of only eleven years he became a child labourer, but educated himself and became a Socialist organizer, married and came to Dublin to continue his work for the Socialist cause. There, among other activities, he founded the Irish Socialist Republican Party in 1896, and, two years later, launched *The Workers' Republic*, a Socialist newspaper. He emigrated to America in 1908 to become an organizer of the Independent Workers of the World and to found there the Irish Socialist Federation as well as to edit the periodical *The Harp*.

10. Slum housing in Cathedral Lane, Dublin, 1904. Although some progress was taking place on the land by the turn of the century, the cities of Ireland, particularly Dublin, had, as had Glasgow, some of the worst living conditions in Europe, not excepting Naples. Nor did Dublin have a vast shipbuilding industry that Belfast and Glasgow enjoyed. Although the British Congested Districts Board brought some alleviation to the chronic economic depression of the western seaboard of both Ireland and Scotland, this did not affect the stagnation in Dublin. It was conditions such as are seen here that fostered the growing labour unrest culminating in the great strike of 1913.

11

11. Major John MacBride, born at Westport, County Mayo in 1869, was the founder and commanding officer of the Irish Brigade, a group of Irish volunteers who fought for the Boer Republics in the South African War. He later became actively involved in Irish Nationalist politics. In 1904 he married Maude Gonne and was the father of the Irish political leader, Sean MacBride. John MacBride served under Commandant MacDonagh in the Irish Volunteers during the 1916 Rising and was executed in Kilmainham Gaol on 5 May of that year.

12

13

12. The City of London Imperial Volunteers marching from Bunhill Row barracks to Nine Elms station to begin their journey to South Africa. The threat of war in South Africa had been intensifying for more than a decade before its outbreak in 1899. The independent sovereign Boer republics of the Orange Free State and the Transvaal, with their rich diamond and gold mining resources, were becoming an ever increasing obstacle to the expansion of the British Cape Colony. Incursions from the Colony eventually resulted in full-scale war. It was the era of 'Jingoism'. 'This war gave a very powerful stimulus to the gathering forces of militant Irish nationalism.

13. Almost 49 years after her previous visit to Ireland, Queen Victoria made a second visit to Dublin in April 1900. The photographs and the film material show that she was given a rousing reception by many Dubliners, and the *Freeman's Journal*, which favoured the Irish Parliamentary Party, now led by John Redmond, and the *Irish Times* which favoured the Unionists, wrote eulogies in her praise. Maude Gonne, however, organized and led a street demonstration in support of the Boers and founded the Irish women's group Inghinidhe na h'Éireann (Daughters of Ireland).

14

14. Arthur Griffith, born in Dublin in 1872, was educated in a Christian Brothers' school in Great Strand Street, before taking work in the office of a Dublin newspaper. An ardent supporter of Parnell, Griffith emigrated to South Africa when the leader of the Irish Parliamentary Party fell. While working as a clerk in the mines, Griffith encountered John MacBride who was a mineral assayer. On the outbreak of the South African War, he returned to Dublin to edit *The United Irishman* and in 1905 he founded the Sinn Fein Party and was drawn further into the struggle for national independence.

15

15. James Daly, Thomas Clarke, two Fenian survivors, and Sean MacDermott, all members of the Irish Republican Brotherhood. This secret oath-bound group was founded in the United States from survivors of the Young Irelanders Rising of 1848 by John O'Mahony and funded by the American Clann na Gael organization. The IRB was the chief instigator of the abortive Fenian Rising of 1867. The failure of that rising did not mean the abandonment of insurrectionary politics by the survivors, many of whom had spent long years of penal servitude in British gaols and prison colonies. The membership of the IRB grew steadily. In the early years of the new century the current of popular feeling in Ireland began to flow more strongly in the direction of nationalism under the influence of such varied writers as John Mitchell, Edward Martyn, George Russell, W.B. Yeats and Padraic Pearse. The swelling IRB membership began to absorb a new generation of activists; Sean MacDermott from County Leitrim, who had been in the United States for some years, became a very active member.

16. Eoin MacNeill, professor of early Irish history at the National University and a Catholic from County Antrim, was the co-founder and vice-president of the Gaelic League, a cultural body founded in 1903 and devoted to the furtherance of the Gaelic language. The other founder was Dr Douglas Hyde, a Protestant scholar and poet, who became its president. The latter individual, who was not a political militant, became the first president of Éire in 1937, while Professor MacNeill was to become the Commander-in-Chief of the Irish Volunteers in 1914.

16

17

17. John Redmond MP, with a cigar; to his left, his son William. Parnell, the great radically inclined leader of the Irish Parliamentary Home Rule Party had been a Protestant landowner. After his fall in 1890, there was considerable disunity in the Irish Parliamentary Party. In 1900, John Redmond, a Catholic landowner became the Party leader and seemed, for a time, to reunite it with the aim of obtaining Dominion status for Ireland, but the aspirations of many were now beginning to turn towards the achievement of an independent nationality for Ireland, not subject to the British Crown nor a part of the Empire.

18. Padraic Pearse, who had an English father and an Irish mother, qualified as a solicitor in 1903 and was appointed editor of the Gaelic League periodical *An Claidmh Sóluis* (the Sword of Light). He was keenly interested in education and very concerned at the British Imperial flavour of education in Ireland, which he felt to be inimical to the Nationalist ethos to which he was strongly committed. To make a beginning in overcoming this influence, he founded a co-educational school called St Enda's. He was soon invited to become a member of the IRB and quickly became one of their leading activists.

18

19. Sir Roger Casement, who came from a County Down family and was to become one of the last 1916 leaders to be executed, had, already by 1912, acquired a reputation as a great humanitarian figure of the order of the Norwegian F. Nansen and the English Florence Nightingale. Serving in the British Consular Service in Africa, he was commissioned to inquire into the rumours of appalling atrocities against native peoples in the Congo Free State, a vast equatorial region personally owned by King Leopold II of Belgium. Casement's report, published in 1903, confirmed that unspeakable injustices and cruelty had been perpetrated, and his work, made known to the world, was eventually instrumental in bringing about King Leopold's surrender of personal ownership of the territory. Casement's later work for the British Consular service was in Brazil, on the Putumayo, where in 1911 he reported on the dreadful exploitation and degradation of native Amazonian Indians for which he received a knighthood. His report, published by order of the British Parliament in 1912, resulted in the British commercial organization which was responsible for the exploitation being forced into liquidation in 1913. Casement then returned to Ireland, throwing himself wholeheartedly into the struggle for Irish independence.

19

20

20. Henry Herbert Asquith MP, and later Earl Oxford and Asquith, became British prime minister under the Liberal administration of 1908. His shaky majority, which the strong opposition of the Conservatives and Unionists rendered increasingly unstable, resulted in Asquith having to call general elections twice in 1910. The outcome of the second election left the 84 members of the Irish Parliamentary Party holding the balance of power. With the aid of the Irish Party members in 1911, Asquith introduced and succeeded in having passed, a bill abolishing the absolute power of veto of the House of Lords, and sought to introduce a modified form of Home Rule legislation. This caused the Unionists, particularly those in the north-east of Ireland to became so alarmed that they decided, with strong support from the Conservative establishment, to take extreme radical action to defend their position within the Union and the Empire.

21. Fianna na h'Éireann boys practise signalling in the Rotunda Gardens, Dublin. This Irish Nationalist youth movement was founded in 1909 by Countess Markievicz, *née* Constance Gore-Booth (*see page 65*), and a prominent place in it was assumed by Liam Mellowes (*third from the left*), who did much to spread its growth throughout the country. It is worth observing that, here too, the uniform of members had a militaristic flavour, but with an American ambiance combined with the Scouting character derived from Sir Robert Smyth's (later Baron Baden-Powell of Gilwell) Boy Scout movement which had been founded the previous year.

21

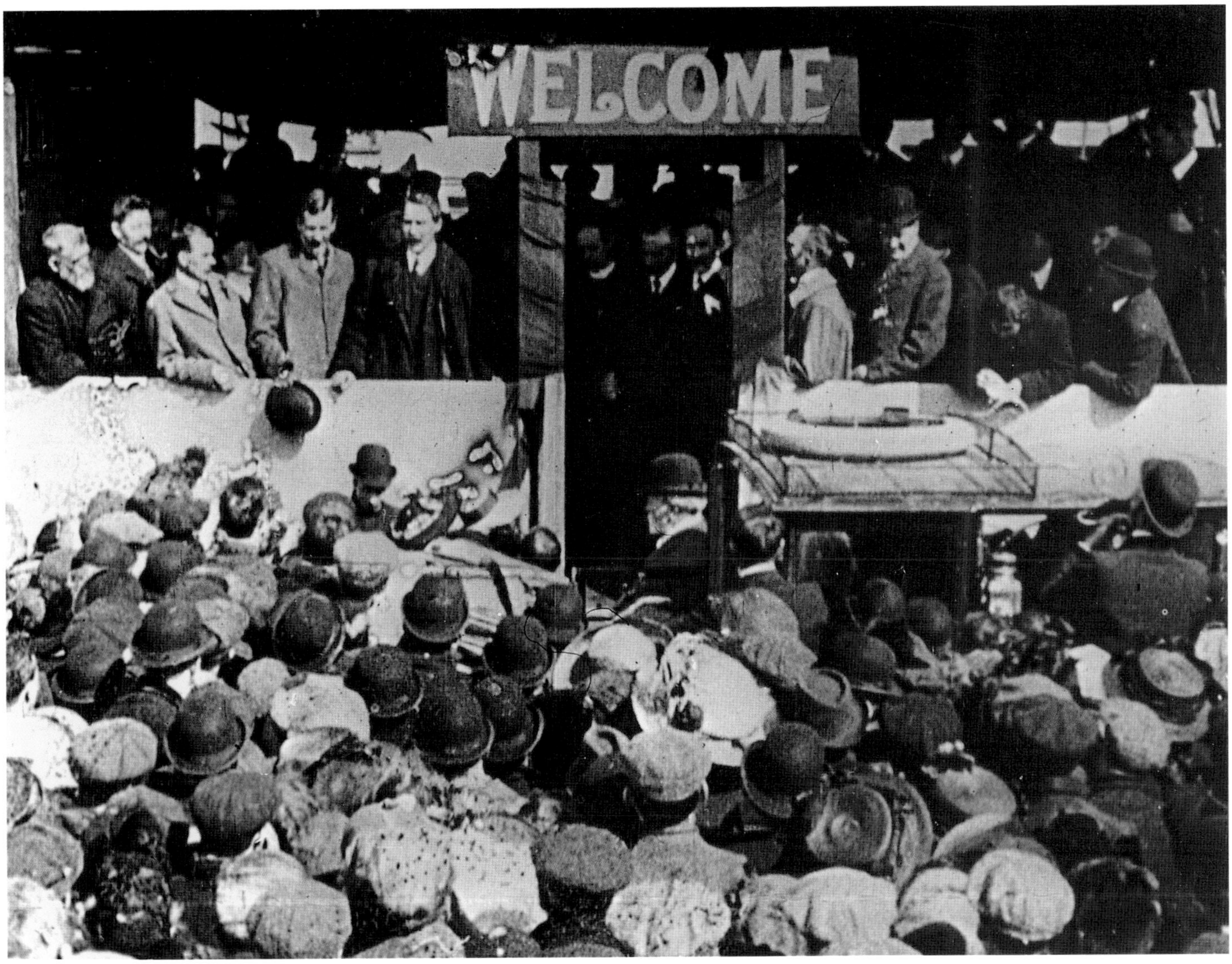

22

22. The Leader of the Conservative Party in England, the Right Honourable Mr Bonar Law, MP (bareheaded, just to the left of the 'Welcome' placard) arrives at the podium at Balmoral, near Belfast, to address a vast concourse of Unionist supporters alarmed by the imminent abolition of the House of Lords' power of veto, on 9 April 1912, just two days before Asquith's Home Rule Bill was due to be put before the House of Commons.

23

23. The grandstand at the Balmoral Show Grounds. At the top right of the photograph are Bonar Law, flanked by the leaders of the Unionist Party, the Marquis of Londonderry (*on his right*) and Sir Edward Carson (*on his left*). Bonar Law, the leader of the British Conservative Party, is about to address a crowd of more than 80,000 Unionist supporters and Orangemen.

24. The crowd before the grandstand listening to Bonar Law. This great gathering was brought about by the fact that the House of Lords' power to veto bills passed in the House of Commons was to be abolished in a bill presented to Parliament in two days' time. In the past this power had allowed the Unionists to prevent the introduction of Home Rule. As Randolph Churchill had done in 1886, Bonar Law now did in 1912; he told the vast gathering 'You hold the pass, the pass for the Empire!' Speeches were also made by Sir Edward Carson and Lord Londonderry, and after these, there was a march past of the assembled multitude.

24

25. A number of the most powerful and distinguished Unionists attending the Balmoral meeting were invited to a house-party at Mount Stewart, the seat of the Marquis of Londonderry, at Strangford Lough, County Down. Here the *gratin* of Northern Unionism assembled to congratulate the British Conservative Party leader and to assure him of their perpetual loyalty. There is a curious atmosphere of triumphalist complacency about this visual document and it is worth identifying the names of those present: (*standing, left to right*) P.G. Cambray; N.W. Apperley; Viscount Boyne; Viscount Castlereagh MP; Lord Claud Hamilton MP; W.F. Montgomery; Master Charles Bonar Law; the Rt Hon Walter H. Long MP; the Rt Hon Sir Robert Finlay KC, MP; Ian Malcolm MP; J.L. Baird MP; and Sir Charles Petrie. (*Sitting, left to right*): the Marquis of Hamilton MP; Viscountess Boyne; the Marquis of Londonderry KG; the Primate of All Ireland; the Marchioness of Londonderry; the Rt Hon Andrew Bonar Law MP; the Rt Hon Sir Edward Carson MP; Viscountess Castlereagh; the Rt Hon Henry Chaplin MP; Admiral Lord Charles Beresford VC, MP. Two faces missing from this gathering are those of the Duke of Abercorn, and Captain (later Sir James) Craig, who became Premier of Northern Ireland and later Lord Craigavon. The gathering of 9 April was quickly followed up with social organization and action. The 12th of July saw what euphemists today would call 'ethnic cleansing'; 2,000 Catholic workmen were driven out of the Belfast shipyards, in spite of the fact that the chairman of Harland & Wolff, Lord Pirrie, was a Liberal and a supporter of Home Rule for Ireland. Bonar Law made another visit to Belfast in July, during which he said 'the Home Rule Bill, in spite of us, may go through the House of Commons. There are stronger things than parliamentary majorities. I can imagine no lengths of resistance to which Ulster will go, in which I shall not be ready to support them and in which they will not be supported by the overwhelming majority of the British people'.

1912

25

26

26. The signals sent by the British Conservative establishment were so unequivocally supportive of the Unionist extremists that the leader of the latter, Sir Edward Carson (*with pen in hand*) launched, on 28 September at Belfast City Hall, the signing of a Solemn League and Covenant declaring that the signatories would be justified '…in using all means which may be found necessary to defeat the present conspiracy to set up a Home Rule Parliament in Ireland. And [sic] in the event of such a Parliament being forced upon us, we further solemnly and mutually pledge ourselves to refuse to recognize its authority.' More than 219,000 signatures were subscribed to this document in the next few months. In December, all those who had signed were asked to enroll for military or political service to oppose Home Rule.

27. Ulster Volunteers drill in Belfast. In December, the Ulster Volunteer Force (UVF) was formed and commenced drilling, at first with wooden staves, but later rifles, as they became available, were substituted. The licences to bear arms were obtained from local magistrates. The secret importation of arms had been going on for some time and a Major Crawford ingeniously contrived to import a number of Vickers machine-guns by bringing them in, stripped down, a piece at a time, over a succession of journeys to and from England.

27

28. A Dublin Metropolitan policeman on the platform of a Dublin tramcar. The year 1913 saw another, though very different, manifestation of social disturbance, this time in Dublin. The proprietor of the *Independent* newspaper, William Martin Murphy, who also owned and controlled a company with a monopoly of the city's tramway services, fell into a dispute with his newspaper and transport employees over their right to union representation by the Irish Transport and General Workers Union, which had been founded in 1909, with James Larkin, a Labour organizer with many years of union experience behind him as General Secretary. Murphy had decided to promote an escalation of the strike through securing the cooperation of the members of the Dublin Employers' Federation. The dispute quickly spread and became a lock-out in which some 400 employers followed Murphy's lead and a third of Dublin's work force was locked out. Magistrates were prevailed upon to prohibit public meetings called by the union and to order their suppression. Dublin Metropolitan policemen were posted on the trams driven by employees intimidated by the threat of dismissal.

29. As the strike spread to the docks, British troops were ordered to undertake the work of striking dockers. Here they are seen unloading a collier at the Coal Quay, some in field uniform, some in fatigue uniform; convoys of carts were driven by and protected by armed soldiers and Royal Irish Constabulary. More and more industrial workers became involved, and in a city where the bitterest poverty was so widespread, the disemployed were quick to feel the helplessness of indigence.

29

28

30

30. Sackville Street (now O'Connell Street), Dublin, 31 August 1913. Public meetings called by the Union were suppressed with violent savagery and raids on the homes of striking workers carried out with great brutality, incurring some loss of life. Here Dublin Metropolitan Police make a baton-charge, intending to break up the meeting that James Larkin had succeeded in addressing by coming to it in disguise, since there was a warrant out for his arrest. Many were seriously injured including innocent bystanders. On another occasion, a girl was shot dead by an armed blackleg. Dublin had never before witnessed such scenes.

31. James Connolly had returned to Ireland from America in 1910. He founded the Irish Labour Party in 1912 and went to Belfast to organize for the Irish Transport and General Workers' Union, coming south at the Union's request to take part in the struggle which continued for months throughout the winter and spring. The official use of overwhelming force against the strikers by the authorities convinced Connolly that organized Labour needed a countervailing force to protect its media outlets and public and private meetings. At a meeting of the Civic League in November 1913, the Irish Citizen Army was born.

31

32

33

32. Imaginative, resourceful and determined, James Larkin became a great Labour leader and an eloquent speaker who drew sympathy for the plight of the Dublin strikers from abroad. The famous Labour pioneer Keir Hardie came to Dublin to lend his support at the funeral of one of the victims and thousands of unionized workers in Britain donated money from their weekly pay packets to buy food for the literally starving strikers, which was dispensed from a soup-kitchen at Liberty Hall organized by Countess Markievicz and Maud Gonne MacBride.

33. The views of many intellectuals began to change – in October 1913, Professor Eoin MacNeill wrote an article for *The Sword of Light* proposing the formation of a body of military volunteers. This idea was actively promoted by the IRB who felt that MacNeill's academic and cultural background would make him a better figurehead to launch such a corps than any of their leading members whose appearance as instigators of such a body would have led to its immediate suppression. A provisional committee was formed without delay under MacNeill's chairmanship.

34

1913

35

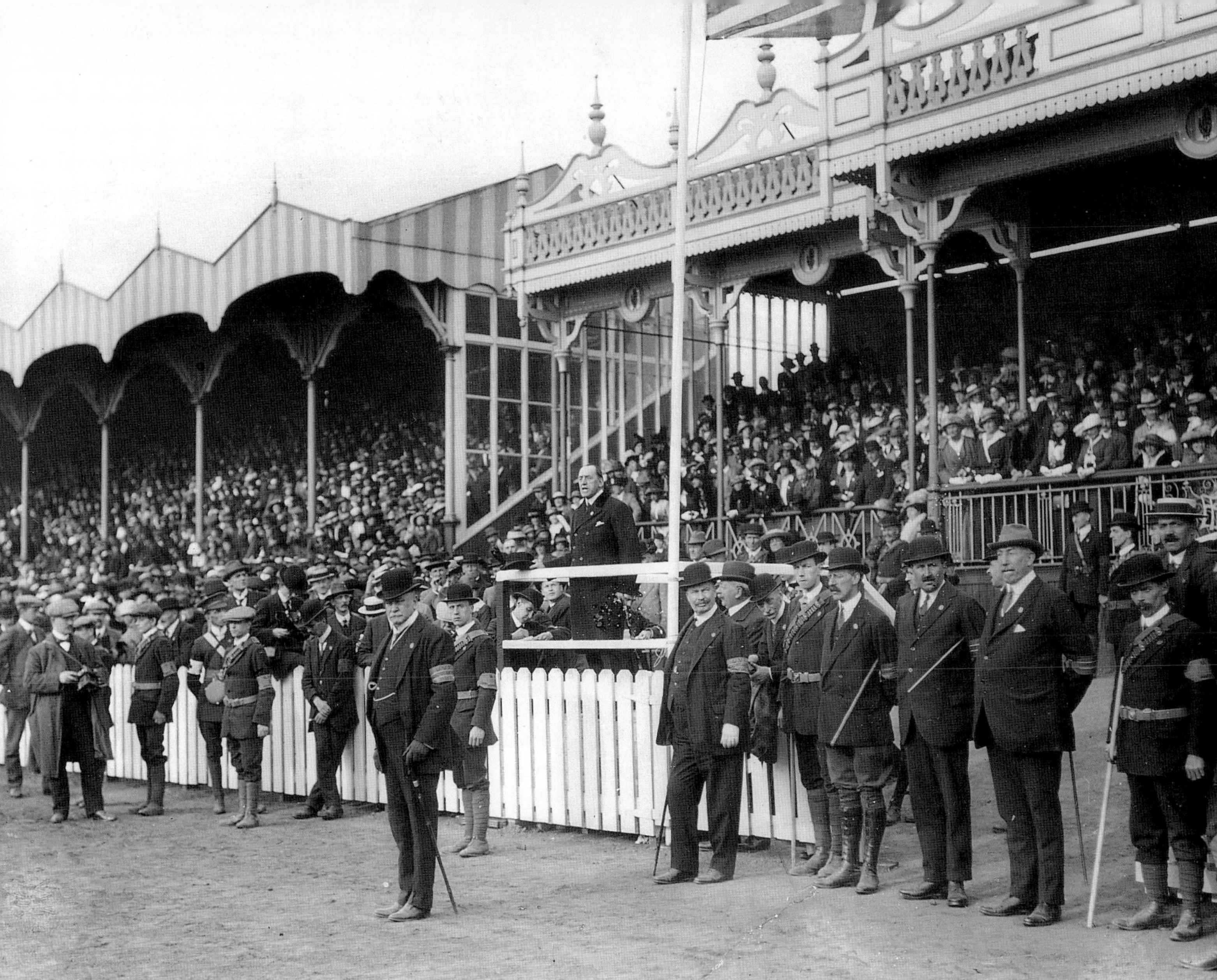

34. The Rotunda, Dublin, where on 25 November 1913, the inaugural meeting of the Volunteers was held. More than 2,000 people attended this first meeting, so that the crowd was forced to overflow into the Rotunda Gardens. Professor MacNeill delivered an address in which he said 'We do not contemplate any hostility to the Volunteer movement that has already been initiated in parts of Ulster. The strength of that movement consists in men whose kinsfolk were among the foremost and the most resolute in winning freedom for the United States of America, in descendants of the Irish Volunteers of 1782, of the United Irishmen of the Antrim and Down insurgents of 1798, of the Ulster Protestants who protested in thousands against the destruction of the Irish Parliament in 1800. The more successful the local Volunteer movement in Ulster becomes, the more completely does it establish the principle that Irishmen have the right to decide and govern their own national affairs'. This speech was much at variance with the views of the Irish Republican Brotherhood (IRB) who were quietly taking over control of the movement. Nine days after the inauguration of the Volunteers, a British Order in Council was made by the government in London prohibiting the import of arms into any part of Ireland.

35. Irish Volunteers drilling with hurley sticks, County Dublin, December 1913. As Asquith's Home Rule Bill was being obstructed, and it became clear that it would not apply to the whole of Ireland nor would it give even Dominion status to a portion of the island, more and more young men turned to the IRB-led Irish Volunteers. By the end of December, companies of the Volunteers like this one were drilling throughout Ireland, using hurley sticks instead of the staves in use by the Ulster Volunteer Force.

36. Sir Edward Carson addressing a mass parade of the Ulster Volunteer Force at Balmoral, in July 1913. In the North, advances in training the UVF had been achieved on account of two salient facts: firstly, a number of British Army generals and scores of highly experienced officers volunteered to serve as instructors, so that skilled training was available at all levels; and secondly, the local oligarchs in north-east Ulster and others throughout the Conservative establishment in England had placed substantial funds into the hands of the UVF for organization, training, manufacture and purchase of transport vehicles, ambulances, uniforms and even, as it was to appear later, for the purchase of arms in very large quantities.

37

37. Sir Edward Carson was the leading figure and guiding genius of this extraordinary political movement, characterized by insurgent opposition to the principles of constitutional parliamentary democracy, yet claiming to support union with Great Britain. In September 1913 he addressed a number of mass meetings of Unionists and at Newry, on 7 September, he declared that a government would be set up which, as soon as the Home Rule Act became law, would take over control of the Province. 'I am told that it will be illegal. Of course it will. Drilling is illegal' and he added, '...the Volunteers are illegal and the Government [he meant the British government] know they are illegal and the Government dare not interfere with them'. Already a middle-aged man at the time of this involvement, he started life as a Dublin Protestant, studied law at Trinity College Dublin, and had had a distinguished career as Irish Solicitor General and as a leading member of the English Bar. He was later appointed to the Privy Council and became Attorney General and a First Lord of Admiralty. When, having eventually been largely instrumental in securing the partition of Ireland, he declined the premiership of Northern Ireland on account of his age, he was made a life peer as Baron Carson of Glencairn and became a Lord of Appeal.

38. The Enniskillen Horse, an intended cavalry wing of the Ulster Volunteer Force (UVF), drill on a private estate in County Fermanagh. Under the overall leadership of General Richardson, an elite cavalry corps called the Enniskillen Horse was formed from among the local landed gentry and more substantial farmers (seen here in training). It looks as though General Richardson had not learned the lessons from the outcome of the battle of Colenso where General Buller lost some of his guns, the battle and his command, in consequence of ordering cavalry armed with lances and swords to charge well-entrenched Boers armed with single-shot Mauser rifles. But generally speaking, the training given the UVF was of a higher standard and much more intensive than that which was possible to give the Volunteers in the South.

39. The UVF Medical Corps was splendidly equipped with expensive ambulances, other transport and tents, a surgical staff and a large body of highly trained nurses. To purchase the equipment and organize a service of this kind was a very expensive undertaking, but it was plain that there was no shortage of money; it came rolling in from many Conservative sources on both sides of the Irish Sea.

38

39

40

40. Another British Conservative leader, the distinguished lawyer F.E. Smith (later Lord Birkenhead), MP for Walton division of Liverpool, came to Ireland to join in the campaign and demonstrate how powerful was the support that the Tory establishment was determined to give to the new movement. On 20 October, while addressing a large crowd at Ballyclare, County Antrim, he said that as soon as the Home Rule Bill became law 'We will say to our followers in England, "To your tents, O Israel!"'. He promised that the Tories would be ready to risk the collapse of the whole body politic to prevent 'this monstrous crime'. Four days later the Ulster Unionist Council declared itself to be 'the Central Authority of the Provisional Government of Ulster'; Sir Edward Carson was appointed chairman and the members included the Duke of Abercorn, the Marquis of Londonderry and Captain James Craig, while the Hon James Campbell KC, MP was made Legal Assessor. An indemnity fund for the support of wounded and disabled members of the UVF and widows and orphans was soon established to the amount of £1 million. That summer Sir Edward Carson lunched with Kaiser Wilhelm II and the outcome of that meeting was to manifest itself in the following spring.

41. The Motorcycle Corps of the Ulster Volunteers, Belfast, April 1914. In April, on behalf of the Provisonal government of Ulster, a chartered steamer, the SS *Mountjoy*, under the direction of Major Crawford and with the cooperation of the German government, brought 35,000 Mauser single-shot rifles and 2.5 million rounds of ammunition, bought in Hamburg with Provisional government funds, through the Kiel Canal, and headed secretly for Larne, in County Antrim. In the darkness of 24 April, the cargo was successfully landed at Larne, Bangor, County Down and at Donaghadee. This was effected with such intense secrecy that none of the cargo was intercepted, but so tight was security that no photographers were allowed to be present and the only visual record is an exceedingly indifferent painting completed after the event. Within hours this huge arms cargo was distributed to previously unarmed Ulster Volunteer Force men all over the North Eastern counties. This photograph, taken near Belfast docks shortly after the event, shows the Motorcycle Corps of the UVF and an infantry section now proudly armed with their Mountjoy rifles. The *de facto* partitioning of Ireland had been secured by the agency of a private army and with overwhelming Tory support, financial and moral.

41

42

43

42. While manœuvering for control of the Volunteer movement in Dublin continued between the IRB faction and John Redmond, a committee was formed in London to plan how arms could be got for the Republican faction of the Volunteers backed by the IRB. The idea of importing rifles and ammunition in yachts was suggested by Mary Spring-Rice and this was taken up enthusiastically by Erskine Childers.

43. Outlawed by the Hague in 1900, this out-of-date ammunition was sold to the Irish Volunteers in 1914 by less than reputable arms dealers.

44

45

44. Although Darryl Figgis failed to give the pre-arranged signal that all was clear, Erskine Childers, after waiting for a little behind Lambay Island, sailed the *Asgard* into Howth harbour and its entire cargo was unloaded in only twenty minutes of highly coordinated work. Here Fianna na h'Éireann boys reach down for rifles. The remaining 600 rifles were landed at Kilcoole, County Wicklow a week later.

45. Mary Spring-Rice helps to get the last of the cargo landed. Although word of the landing had reached Dublin Castle, and police and troops blocked the road into Dublin, they captured only nineteen of the rifles. The Irish Volunteers scattered and hid the arms for later recovery. Word of the failure of the forces of the Crown to get many of the guns was all over Dublin in a few hours and a company of King's Own Scottish Borderers, marching to barracks via Bachelors Walk in the centre of Dublin were jeered and stoned by a crowd. The officer in charge panicked and ordered his men to fire on the crowd, rusulting in three deaths and 32 injuries.

46

46. Mrs Reddin, a prominent leader in the militant women's organization, Cumann na m'Bán (driving a dog-cart) leads their contingent at the funerals of the last of the victims of the Bachelors Walk shooting. All the victims were given what were virtually state funerals, in which city officials, Irish Volunteers and the Irish Citizen Army, fully armed with Howth rifles, participated in large contingents. The IRB could not have imagined that an event so much to their purpose would have occurred, and indeed the tragedy united all classes in Dublin as these deaths were the first blood shed in the Irish struggle for independence in the twentieth century.

47

1914–15

47. Uniformed and armed with Howth rifles, a contingent of the Irish Citizen Army parades in front of Liberty Hall, September 1914. World War I had begun and the deflated Home Rule Bill had been indefinitely suspended. With James Connolly as its commander, the Irish Citizen Army, recruited from trades unionists in the previous year, declared its determination to have no part in what it regarded as a capitalist conflict, pledging itself to the fight for Irish independence in cooperation with the IRB-led faction of the Volunteers, now called the Irish Volunteers.

48. John Redmond, leader of the Irish Parliamentary Party (*on the left*), was still struggling to gain control of the Volunteer movement, but three weeks after this photograph was taken the movement split. The smaller portion adhered to the IRB-led Irish Volunteers and were given Howth rifles; the remainder became known as the National Volunteers and continued to support Redmond. The numbers of the latter declined as they joined the British Army in response to the recruiting drives for World War I. The IRB-led Irish Volunteers continued their military training.

48

49. Unlike the Unionist Ulster Volunteers, the Irish Volunteers had very few professional soldiers to provide them with training. The meagre funding that was available for equipping them with uniforms had to be eked out by small weekly contributions from the Volunteers themselves; as a result the majority never actually had full uniforms, even when they finally went into action a year after this photograph was taken.

50. A Dublin tramcar adapted as a mobile recruiting office for the Royal Dublin Fusiliers in Dame Street, June 1915. The appalling waste of life in the World War led to an ever-increasing demand for men, and although many who had remained in Redmond's National Volunteers had joined the British Army, their numbers represented only a tiny sop to the insatiable maw of World War. Prime Minister Asquith decided to come to Dublin to address a large recruiting meeting in the Mansion House. This event almost led to a premature triggering of the now inevitable rising, for the Irish Citizen Army and the Irish Volunteers made a coordinated plan to seize the Mansion House in order to prevent the meeting taking place, but they were pre-empted by superior numbers of Crown forces occupying it and the action was cancelled.

49

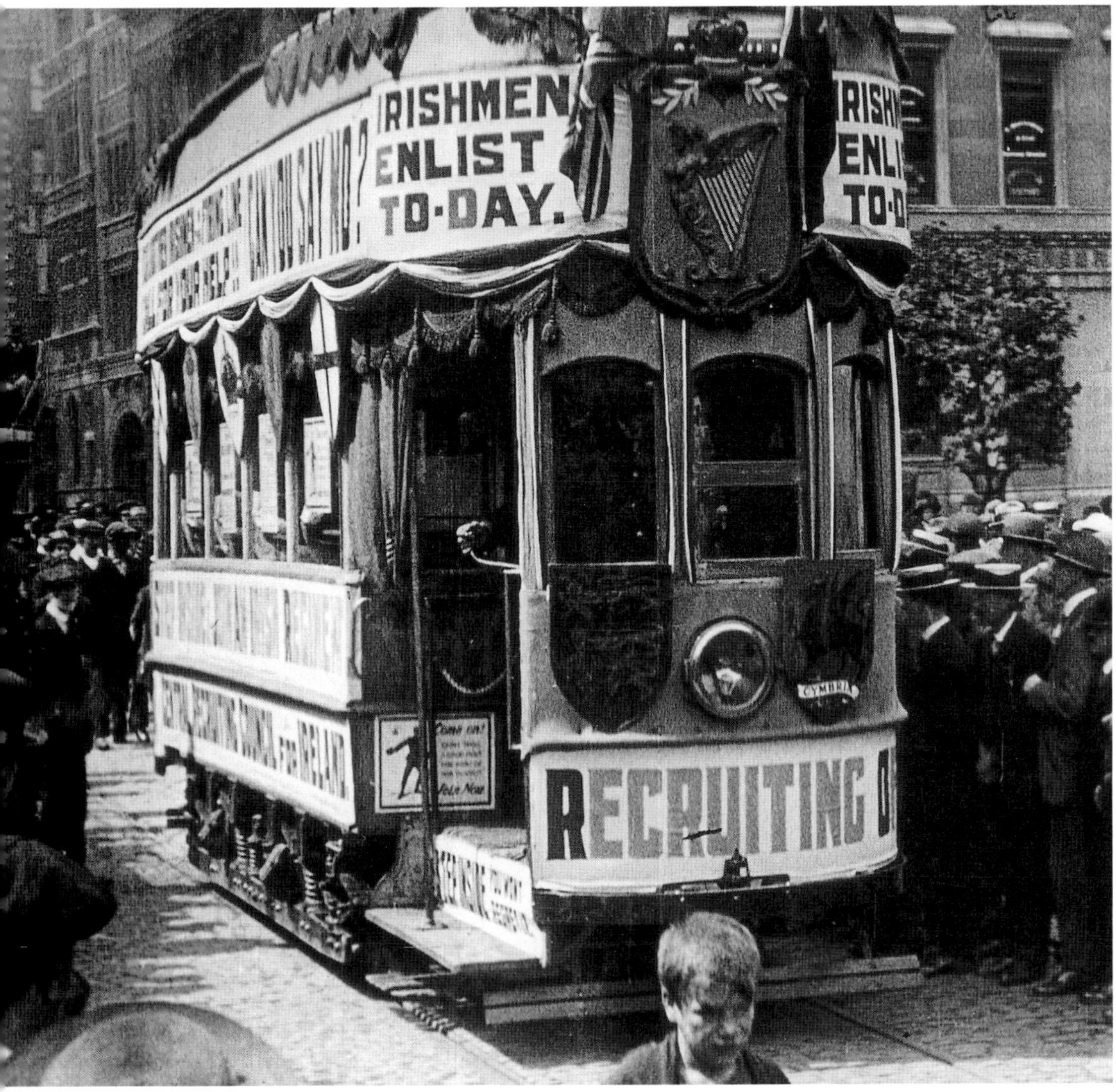

50

FIGHT
FOR
RELAND,

51. In this recruiting parade for the Royal Dublin Fusiliers it is interesting to see the propaganda slogan 'Fight for Ireland' carried on the banner, introduced on what turned out in the event to be a tenuous assumption that the war was being fought 'for the freedom of small nations'. How this aspiration was to be applied to Ireland was demonstrated in 1919, at the Versailles Conference (*see page 105*).

52. Though their numbers were small, the equipment and training of the Irish Citizen Army were superior to that of most of the Irish Volunteers because they had trades union money behind them and, consequently, full uniforms and a full-time, well-trained professional soldier to instruct them. He was none other than the only son of General Sir George White of White Hall in County Antrim, the British Commander of the defence of Ladysmith in the South African War. Six feet two inches tall, Captain Jack White is to be seen at the left of the photograph, bearing one of the flags. The author recalls him from a memory of early childhood as a gentle giant whose sensitive good manners were extended to children as well as to adults.

52

53

54

53. In furtherance of his work for the IRB, Sir Roger Casement went first to New York and from there to Germany, to seek, as Sir Edward Carson had done, for arms, and also to attempt to form an Irish Legion from among Irishmen captured as prisoners-of-war. He was successful in increasing the number of arms to be sent, but could get few recruits for his Irish Legion. Throughout his visit to Germany, he was accompanied by a British secret agent by the name of Beverley, who was using the pseudonym of Bailey.

54. Joseph Plunkett. Count Plunkett's family and he himself were all entirely committed to the Republican cause. From 1914, Plunkett, a minor poet with a good command of French and German, acted as an undercover diplomatic agent for the IRB, journeying between Ireland, New York and Germany. This is his passport picture. Throughout most of his short life he suffered from crippling ill health. On his return to Ireland in 1915, he was hospitalized but his conscience would not allow him to remain in hospital when the Rising came. He was executed on 4 May 1916, having been married on the previous evening to Miss Grace Gifford in the tiny chapel in Kilmainham Gaol, after which they were allowed one hour together.

55

55. It is understandable that all this militarism should be reflected in the children's games of the time, as may be seen in this photograph taken in Beresford Place, near Liberty Hall, Dublin. Just as the more privileged boys were encouraged to dress as soldiers, so these poor, bare-footed boys have made themselves into soldiers as best they can. We are looking at a theme which has been repeated continuously over the years in Irish life, both North and South.

56. Padraic Pearse, with bared and bowed head (*upper left in profile*) about to give his famous oration at the graveside of O'Donovan-Rossa, the great Fenian leader, in Glasnevin Cemetery in 1915. Here he said 'While Ireland holds these graves, Ireland, unfree, shall never be at peace'. The funerals of the victims of the Bachelors Walk shooting and that of Jeremiah O'Donovan-Rossa were, after the abysmal foundering of Asquith's mutilated Home Rule Bill, the most potent factors in generating wide public support for resistance, even by force, to British Imperial dominance. The North had shown that the insurrection of privilege and power could defy the British Parliament with impunity. But there was no correspondingly powerful faction in England to support a struggle for an independent Republic of Ireland. Republicans would have to achieve this by themselves and with resources that might come to them from Irish America. The name of Arthur Griffith's political party, Sinn Fein (By Ourselves) had come to have a particularly evocative significance. An armed insurrection which would proclaim an Irish Republic was about to take place.

56

57. On 12 April, Sir Roger Casement set out aboard the German naval submarine *U19* with the intention of being put ashore on the West Coast of Ireland. His efforts to form an Irish Legion had failed, nor had he succeeded in getting anything like the quantity of arms sent to Ireland that he had hoped for. A sick man, he was still accompanied by Beverley, the British agent who was instructed to follow him and who stands behind his left shoulder; on Beverley's left, leaning over the rail is Robert Monteith, a member of the Irish Legion. Casement landed successfully on Banna Strand, Ballyheigue Bay, County Kerry, to be immediately betrayed, captured, brought to the Tower of London, tried as a traitor and sentenced to death. A British Knight, he had conspired with the Germans to obtain illegal arms from them and was hanged at Pentonville.

58. The ruins in Sackville Street, opposite the General Post Office, Dublin, which had been the headquarters of the Republican forces in the 1916 Rising. From the moment they marched out together, the Irish Citizen Army and the Irish Volunteers ceased to be separate bodies and became the Irish Republican Army. The leaders were aware that what they were undertaking would lead to military defeat, but would result in an overwhelming mass psychological victory. It would be impossible for the British government to restore the political status quo, and there would be no turning back the clock. After many previous attempts the IRB had succeeded in precipitating an event that would prove to be historically crucial.

57

58

59

59. Under prisoners' escort, Commandant Michael Mallin and (*on his left*) Lieutenant Constance Markievicz, second in command, both in Irish Citizen Army uniform, at Ship Street Barracks near Dublin Castle, after the surrender of their contingent at the College of Surgeons. Mallin was sentenced to death and was executed at Kilmainham Goal. But Madame Markievicz had her death sentence commuted to life imprisonment. She was the first serving woman combat officer of the twentieth century. She was later to be the first woman to be elected to the British Parliament.

60

61

60. Commandant Eamon de Valera, in Irish Volunteer officer's uniform under prisoners' escort at the time of his court martial. De Valera was the only commandant of the Rising not to be executed. Much speculation has been devoted over the years to arrive at an explanation for this. It has been suggested that his American citizenship may have been one reason, but there were also other factors that must be taken into account.

61. Michael Collins, seen here in Irish Volunteer officer's uniform. As a young man from Clonakilty, County Cork, he had been obliged to emigrate to get work in London in the service of the Post Office, then had returned to Dublin before the Rising. He became a member of the IRB and an Irish Volunteer officer and served with distinction in the Republican headquarters during the fighting. Together with other serving officers of the IRA who had not been executed, he was sentenced to a long term of imprisonment and interned at Frongoch Camp in North Wales. His work in the postal service made him realize the critical importance of communications and intelligence, and while in prison formulated the idea of a special service. This group became known as the Black Hand and formed the nucleus of the intelligence service.

62

62. The harsh realities of modern warfare in the heart of their city came as a profound shock to ordinary Dubliners, making it hard to take in what was happening, but gradually, as the executions and internments continued, there began a political reorientation which would not begin to manifest itself publicly throughout Ireland until some months had passed. To the right in the photograph, across O'Connell Street, is the ruined shell of the Imperial Hotel, where from a first floor window Jim Larkin had addressed the crowd during the 1913 strike.

63. Joseph Plunkett's workroom in his father's house, Larkfield, Kimmage, Dublin, after a raid by British intelligence men in 1916. Joseph Plunkett had been concerned with intelligence matters during the build up to the Rising. The executions, raids and internments had demolished the structures that would be urgently needed for the continuance of the struggle for national independence. These structures would have to be built up all over again and it was fortunate that a man with the abilities of the young Michael Collins was to be motivated to play a leading part in this essential task.

63

The operation of a civil administration, law courts and a civil police force is utterly dependent on the voluntary acquiescence of the population of the area concerned in the operation of those institutions. Where this is withheld by the population, or even by a large portion of it, and their allegiance is transferred to an alternative administration, civil administration and civil policing become impossible and coercion must be resorted to if the regime is determined to hold on to power. This, through an escalating series of para-military stages, culminates in war and the implementation of martial law. It is just such a tragic train of events which began to unfold in Ireland.

64. On 11 November 1919, the anniversary of Armistice Day, Field Marshall Viscount French staged a victory parade in Dublin. Peace was not the prevailing motif created by this display of massed troops and armour. The atmosphere intended was one of overwhelming military might against which the puny efforts of the Irish Nationalists could not hope to prevail. After its defeat in the Easter Rising, the Republican ideal was now to be embodied in a popularly elected legislature sitting in Dublin. Unlike the alternative government established in the North, the British authorities were determined to destroy tthe Dublin government by force.

The Tan War

Shift in civil allegiance

Gofasta
Golikell
FANNYS SISTER

65

65. The exercise yard, Stafford Gaol, early spring, 1917. The very large numbers of prisoners resulting from the courts martial were more than the existing prison system in both England and Ireland could cope with, so that prison camps had to be opened in many different places. They quickly became open universities where Irish and other languages, and Irish history were studied; but they also became universities of insurrection and training establishments for the continued struggle that was now clearly inevitable.

66. By the spring of 1917 the change in public attitudes was beginning to be seen, led in the absence of so many of the participants by the Labour movement, as this banner on the partially rebuilt Liberty Hall indicates. Many Irish and even English artists and intellectuals had begun to express opinions quite at variance with the British Establishment's view that those who took part in the Easter Rising were traitors. As they occurred, the by-elections in 1917 in many parts of Ireland were contested and all but one were won by Sinn Fein candidates (the exception was that of Armagh South). Count Plunkett, returned as the Sinn Fein candidate, refused to take his seat at Westminster, as did all the other Sinn Fein candidates elected.

66

1917

67

67. Members of the new British Prime Minister Lloyd George's National Convention meeting at Trinity College Dublin on 25 June 1917. It had become clear to the wartime coalition government in London that the situation in Ireland had changed in a very fundamental way. The old system was finished but what was to go in its place? It was clear to the new Prime Minister that the mutilated and discredited Home Rule Bill was a non-starter. He felt the urgent need for some political device to divert the growing surge towards Republicanism, and offered two proposals: a Council of Ireland, which could not be agreed upon; and the setting up of an Irish National Convention where all shades of opinion could debate the question of what was to be the future of Ireland. It was intended that this latter body be no more than a discussion group, the outcome of whose debate might or might not influence the decisions of the British government. Sinn Fein rejected the idea out of hand and boycotted the National Convention completely. Only two men of Republican sympathies attended: the agriculturist, painter and writer George Russell (A.E.) (the bearded man wearing a hat at the back of the group), and Erskine Childers (not in this picture), who became secretary of the Convention.

68. In order to secure an Irish public reaction favourable to the National Convention, the British government arranged to release a number of Republican prisoners, the first of them arriving in Dublin on the morning of 17 June, to scenes of enthusiastic welcome. Here the welcoming crowds are seen in Brunswick Street (now Pearse Street) adjoining Westland Row. Constance Markievicz arrived by the evening boat to scenes of mass enthusiasm such as had never before been witnessed in Dublin.

68

1917

69

69. Constance Markievicz, seen here in her Cumann na m'Bán uniform, shortly after her return to Dublin from Aylesbury Prison. Once the heavy retouching of this photograph was removed, it was very evident that the enormous stress of the previous four years had left its impress on her beautiful face. It shows also that her sensitivity and great-heartedness were undiminished and that her staunchness and determination were as present as ever. As one would have expected, she flung herself once again into the fight for the Republican cause, organizing the struggle through the Cumann na m'Bán and the Sinn Fein Party. Though much weakened in health, a health she was never fully to regain, she spoke at almost every by-election and general election that took place, as well as on many other occasions to different groups. Constance Markievicz was the first woman to be elected an MP, was to suffer imprisonment again, both at the hands of the British and the Irish authorities, and yet never lost her warmth and her love of ordinary people whom she made her companions for the remainder of her life. It is very understandable that she became, at last, a great national heroine.

70

70. The only surviving IRA commandant of the 1916 Rising, Eamon de Valera, speaking at the 1917 Kilkenny by-election on behalf of the Sinn Fein candidate, Alderman William T. Cosgrave, who was to be returned with twice the number of votes than were given to the Irish Parliamentary Party candidate. Cosgrave had been sentenced to death for his part in the Easter Rising but his sentence had been commuted. The harshness of British political and military pressure had united, as nothing else could have done, the extraordinary diversity of outlook that characterized the membership of the Sinn Fein Party at this time. Cosgrave was returned and, like the other Sinn Fein members elected, (including de Valera, who had won the East Clare by-election), waited to participate in the work of an Irish National Legislature in Dublin.

71. Members of the special group known as the Black Hand, selected and trained by Michael Collins in Frongoch Internment Camp, were photographed after their release. Collins had become convinced of the essential importance of forming an active communications and intelligence staff and as soon as he was released, he undertook this task as a matter of the first priority. Without Collins's foresight and determined action in this field the turn of events in the next few years could have been quite different from that which transpired. Though one is glad that such a document as this photograph survives, one cannot but be surprised at the action of this group in arranging for themselves to be photographed, since such photographs were the occasion of many disasters to units of this sort.

71

72

73

72. In August, Thomas Ashe, a young traditional musician, was arrested and charged with making speeches 'calculated to cause disaffection'. An active Irish Volunteer, he had been imprisoned for life in 1916, but released in June 1917. After the most recent arrest he was imprisoned in Mountjoy Gaol, Dublin, where IRA prisoners were protesting at being treated as common criminals and were demanding prisoner-of-war status. When their demands were not met, they went on hunger-strike. The Lord Mayor of Dublin, Lawrence O'Niell, visited the prisoners and found that Ashe was without bedding and had been brutally treated while being force-fed. Ashe collapsed during another session of force-feeding and was taken to the nearby Mater Hospital where he died five hours later. His death was the first of many such deaths in similar circumstances. An inquest recorded that his death had been caused by the brutal treatment received from prison authorities. It also condemned force-feeding and recorded the fact that the Prisons Board refused to give evidence or to hand over documents. Ashe was given the equivalent of a state funeral and the oration at his graveside was delivered by Michael Collins, the first occasion on which Collins took a leading part in a public event.

73. Field Marshal Sir John Denton Pinkstone French (later Earl of Ypres), in the grounds of the Vice-Regal Lodge, Dublin, on his appointment as Lord-Lieutenant General and General Governor of Ireland. On 16 April 1918, the British Parliament passed an act to introduce conscription into Ireland. The appointment of a military supremo whose policy would be to enforce conscription was a sinister augury of the times about to begin. On his appointment to Ireland, the Field Marshall had said 'Home Rule will be offered and declined, then conscription will be enforced. If they leave me alone I can do what is necessary'.

75

74. A gathering in Dublin makes the Anti-Conscription Declaration. Field Marshall French had underestimated the difficulties which lay ahead for the conscription issue. A one-day country-wide general strike was called by the trades unions, during which great numbers of men and women made the Anti-Conscription Declaration at the Mansion House and elsewhere throughout Ireland, and signed a pledge to resist conscription. It was estimated that for every division of conscripts got out of the island, two divisions of British troops would have to be put in. The act was allowed to lapse, the war which had led to its enactment had come to an end by mid-November and a general election was due in December.

75. It is doubtful if any general election in Ireland, before or since, aroused quite as much public interest, but before canvassing could effectively begin, on the slimmest of evidence, a charge of a 'German Plot' had been made to excuse the arbitrary arrest under emergency powers still in force of 73 of the Sinn Fein potential candidates. The result was a landslide victory for Sinn Fein, which, coincidentally, had 73 candidates returned. The 'German Plot' manoeuvre had been a political disaster.

74

76

1919

76. Dublin Metropolitan police keeping order outside the entrance to the Round Room of the Mansion House on the afternoon of the 21 January 1919. All the Sinn Fein members returned in the general election had pledged their constituents not to take their seats at Westminster but to assemble in Dublin and establish an independent Republican National Parliament to be know as Dail Éireann. They were all elected MPs and, thereby theoretically free from arrest, but many, arrested as suspects in the so-called 'German Plot', had just been freed from prison as the result of their election, including Constance Markievicz.

77. At 3.30 pm those Dail members not in prison assembled in the Round Room. Of the 73 returned as TDs (Members of the Dail), 36 of these, including the president of Sinn Fein, Eamon de Valera and Arthur Griffith, were still incarcerated. None of the non-Republican returned candidates was present. It was Count Plunkett who proposed that on account of this, Cathal Brugha should preside. Father O'Flanagan, who was later to be excommunicated for refusing to deny absolution to dying Republicans read a short prayer in Irish, the Clerks of the Day were appointed and the Roll was called. The Provisional Constitution of the Dail was read and passed unanimously. Then all present stood up and Ireland's Declaration of Independence was read. Among other business transacted that day was the appointment of delegates to the Peace Conference at Versailles. There were no attempts to interrupt the proceedings, nor were any of those present arrested; the day in Dublin passed peacefully. In Soloheadbeag, County Tipperary, however, the first shots in what would be a long guerrilla war were fired when a group of IRA men captured a load of dynamite and shot dead two Royal Irish Constabulary men who were guarding the explosive.

77

78

78. Recruitment to the IRA and training continued, for it was evident that a prolonged struggle was about to begin and that the Dail could not count on being able to continue its business in public. The response of the British to the incident at Soloheadbeag had been the proclamation of County Tipperrary as a military area under the Defence of the Realm Regulations; very soon other counties were added to the list of areas under military rule.

79. Due to the fact that those originally chosen to be delegates to Versailles were still in gaol, Alderman Sean T. O'Kelly TD (later President of Éire) and lawyer George Gavan Duffy (later to be one of the Ministers Plenipotentiary in the Treaty negotiations) were sent to the Peace Conference by order of the Dail, but to no avail. The four principal powers had agreed that no country could be admitted to the hearings unless their admission were unanimously approved beforehand.

79

80

80. Constance Markievicz caring for the O'Carroll children whose father and mother were in prison. The disruption of children's lives is one of the saddest aspects of social disturbance and one that has a prolonged destabilizing effect on the social fabric, from generation to generation.

81. Field Marshall Viscount French in his capacity as Governor-General, takes the salute at the saluting-base outside the Bank of Ireland. Having failed over conscription and at the polls in Ireland, the coalition government, with very active Tory support, was preparing to enforce British Sovereignty by might against the democratically elected separatist Republican Dail and crush its civil service and army. French was seen by the coalition government in London to be a suitable governor to oversee the enforcement of this policy.

81

82. In the escalating effort to destabilize the Republican administrative structure, more and more use was made of the Crown Forces as the combination of Royal Irish Constabulary, Dublin Metropolitan Police, Special Branch, Secret Service and regular Army troops came to be known. Armoured cars and soldiers with fixed bayonets in the streets became commonplace. In this photograph two of the types of armoured car employed are seen. To the left, the Rolls-Royce 'Whippet' carrying a Vickers machine-gun in an armoured rotating turret which could turn through 360°, and on the right, the 'Peerless' armoured car which carried two turrets each containing a Hotchkiss machine-gun, each turret having a rotation of 320°. The 'Peerless' was an exceedingly heavy and rather clumsy vehicle with solid tyres, not having the speed and manoeuverability of the 'Whippet'.

83. The 'Regular' soldiers had been prepared for combat duty in the World War and had neither adequate training nor aptitude for police work. Most of them had a particular dislike of this work and the even more repugnant work of the Special Branch. It was hardly surprising then that morale was very low. Over-stretched, inadequate and ineffective in destroying the Dail administration as they were, the Crown Forces in Ireland were costing the British taxpayer some £10,800,000 a year, a staggering sum in those days. The British administration decided to set up two other bodies of what were, in effect, a *schutzstaffel* of militarized police, that would be recruited from demobilized soldiers. The first, open to 'other ranks', was to be paid, in modern terminology, fifty pence a day; the second body, drawn from demobilized officers, was offered a hundred pence a day; both were to be loosely attached to the Royal Irish Constabulary.

84. A Dail (Irish Parliament) Commission in session. On 10 September, the British administration declared the Dail a dangerous organization and orders for its suppression were given, but it continued its work in secret. Seen here is a session of the Dail Commission of Inquiry into the Industrial Resources of Ireland, meeting in secret at Dublin City Hall on 29 November 1919. A complete rethink of the economy of the country was envisaged and its natural resources were surveyed by this commission, agriculture being regarded as an industry. As well as this, the Dail set up Courts of Justice, Land Arbitration Courts and an unarmed Republican Police Force to keep order. Every department of government was mirrored in the civil administration organized by the appropriate commissions of the Dail. But unlike the alternative regime set up in Belfast, the forces of the Crown were actively deployed to destroy the organs of the Republican Dail and to annihilate its growing power.

82

83

84

85.The first Black and Tans being inspected by a Royal Irish Constabulary officer at Beggars Bush Barracks, Dublin, on their arrival on 25 March 1920. Because of an acute shortage of uniforms and the overriding need to cut expenses in every possible way, their uniform consisted of war-surplus khaki jackets, black trousers and black 'Glengarry' hats, although in this picture they are dressed in the same colour top and bottom. Each was issued with a service revolver and, at times, with a rifle. It has been asserted that many were socially maladjusted as a consequence of their wartime service and had difficulties in adapting to peace-time life. The dreadful record for indiscipline and drunkenness which they acquired seems to bear this out.

86. The head office of the Sinn Fein bank in Dublin after a raid by the Black and Tans. The alternative administration's financial institutions were targeted by the British administration; as a result the Sinn Fein bank was forced to carry on its activities in secret, using a large number of accounts belonging to private individuals which made it extremely hard to trace. Michael Collins, as Minister for Finance, had successfully launched two loans which were quickly oversubscribed and honoured to the last penny.

87. British soldiers leaving a driverless train at Kingsbridge station in Dublin, April 1920. Irish trade unionists also played their part in resistance to coercion. Train crews refused to work trains carrying British soldiers and munitions and, when compelled to do so under the Defence of the Realm Act, the crews worked to rule in a manner which made it almost impossible to secure convictions other than by Courts Martial in the counties under Martial Law.

88. Black and Tans and Auxilliaries raiding the Gaelic Athletic Association's premises, Dublin. In wet weather, Army waterproof trenchcoats were worn over the pied uniform, but all the Black and Tans can be distinguished from the 'pound-a-day' men by the fact that the Black and Tans were 'other ranks' and wore puttees, while the group drawn from demobilized officers, called the 'Auxilliaries' wore dark tunics and trousers with tall boots or leather leggings. The Black and Tans are carrying away the curved hurling sticks used for playing the traditional Irish game of hurley. As we have seen on page 80, these sticks were frequently used in drilling when rifles were not available.

85

86

87

89

89. A crowd watches as British soldiers and RIC Auxilliaries drive away arrested Sinn Fein suspects in a Dublin street. The hunt for the executives of the Republican government departments and the commanding officers of the IRA intensified. Lorry-loads of troops and Auxilliaries supported by armoured cars and tanks took part in these raids, which were more frequent by night. But before raids of this kind could effectively be carried out, knowledge of the identity, function, habits and addresses of these individuals had to be obtained. For almost a century the Royal Irish Constabulary had been one of the prime sources of information of this kind, but they were now socially isolated and their usefulness as a source of tactical information had lessened. The Crown Forces now had urgent need of new sources of information.

90. The 'Cairo Gang'. Groups of special secret-service men were clandestinely recruited in England and infiltrated into Ireland. These and Special Branch men of the DMP and RIC became the targets of Collins's counter-intelligence service which was now highly organized with agents and contacts within the postal and telephone services; there were contacts even in Dublin Castle itself supplying Collins with information.

1920

90

92

91. Thomas MacCurtain, Lord Mayor of Cork. By now, many of the lord mayors, aldermen and city officials in most of the cities in Ireland were, at least, Sinn Fein supporters, if not actually civil servants of the Dail government or high-ranking officers in the IRA. Thomas MacCurtain was all of these, but in order to fulfil his work as a public official he had, like many of the others, to reside at a known address. Such men, as sitting targets, were exposed to almost unendurable stress; and their steadfastness and fortitude in the carrying out of their duties were of enormous value to the morale of all those committed to the struggle for independent nationhood. On 19 March, in a brief engagement with the IRA, a RIC constable was shot dead near Cork. Those controlling the operations of the Crown Forces decided upon a reprisal. As darkness fell, British troops and RIC men surrounded the area where MacCurtain's home was situated. They turned away the lamplighters so that the streets were in darkness and prevented any public access. Then a squad of plainclothes Royal Irish Constabulary with blackened faces broke into MacCurtain's house and shot him dead.

92. Unarmed Republican police hold back a large crowd demonstrating in sympathy with hunger-strikers in Mountjoy Goal, Dublin in April 1920. The Republican government had not neglected the need for civil policing and had formed a highly efficient force of unarmed police for crowd control, traffic duties and all the activities of a normal civil police force. The decision that the force should be unarmed was a momentous one, for it established the precedent followed by the Civic Guards in 1922 and by our present-day police, the Garda Siochána (guardians of the peace).

91

93

94

1920

93. Crowds outside Mountjoy Gaol during the hunger-strikes of April 1920. As in 1917, when the prison authorities tried to mix Republican prisoners with criminals and to give them a similar prison regime, the Republicans called a hunger-strike in protest. This time no attempt was made at force-feeding, but as the strikers got weaker the crowds outside the prison grew, and notices of sympathy were posted up on the very doors of the gaol. World-wide sympathy made it impossible for Lloyd George to ignore the situation; eventually the Republicans were given prisoner-of-war status and the hunger-strike was called off.

94. As the status of the Republican prisoners changed to that of prisoners-of-war, and the hunger-strike ended, many of the hunger-strikers were transferred to Dublin hospitals. The arrival of these prisoners in the Mater Hospital, Dublin, was the occasion of an enormous peaceful demonstration of sympathy. Scenes such as these, reported and illustrated in the world's press, created much support for the struggle for independence.

95. One of the hunger-strikers, Phillip Shanaghan, recovering in hospital. When they had regained their strength, the prisoners were returned to gaol to continue their sentences, but were segregated from the criminal prisoners and allowed to elect their own representatives and have the other privileges usually associated with prisoners-of-war.

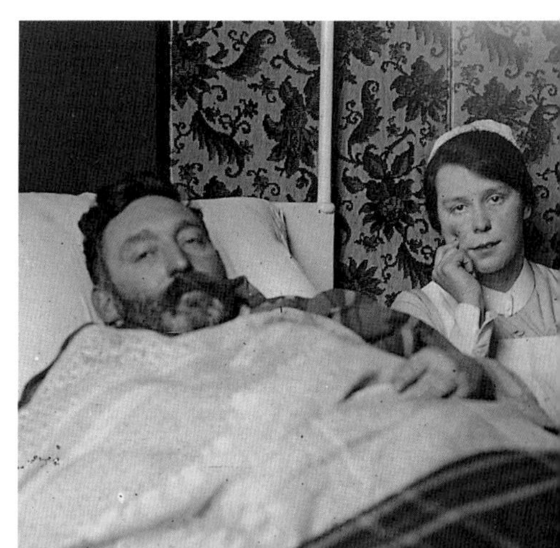

95

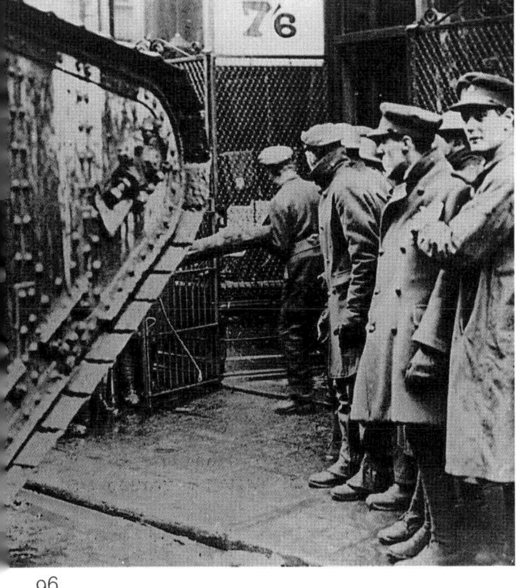

96

98

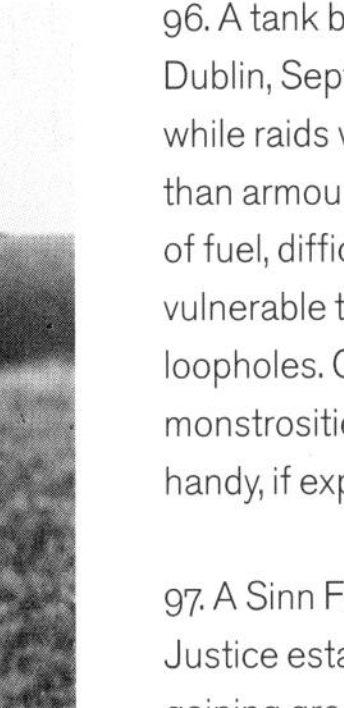

97

96. A tank being used to force a door in Parnell Street, Dublin, September 1920. Used to support Crown Forces while raids were carried out, they proved less efficient than armoured cars or lorries. They were also wasteful of fuel, difficult to manoeuvre and maintain, and were vulnerable to attack from gunfire through their loopholes. One use was found for these military monstrosities, already obsolete in the field; they were handy, if expensive, for forcing metal grilles and doors.

97. A Sinn Fein judge of the Land Court. The Courts of Justice established by the Dail extended their influence, gaining ground on the courts of the British regime. This was particularly so in respect of the Land Arbitration Courts, set up by the Dail to settle disputes over questions of land ownership and use. Although these courts sometimes had to give verdicts in favour of some of the larger landlords, their decisions enjoyed a high degree of acceptance as being equitable, especially as the judges were often local people conversant with local history and conditions. The judges of the Land Courts were, like the lord mayors of the cities, particularly vulnerable to clandestine attack. This particular judge, a dairy farmer, was shot dead six weeks after this photograph was published.

98. An IRA 'flying column' in County Tipperary. Antithetical to the lumbering steel dinosaurs designed for breaching lines of trenches, were the light, mobile, 'flying columns' of highly trained guerrilla fighters that the IRA was now able to put in the field in greater numbers. There were now very considerable areas of the countryside where the British administration had completely broken down. The men of the 'flying columns', hidden in friendly farmhouses or living in concealed camps and dug-outs, had become experienced at forced marches and mobile tactics. Being protected by a sympathetic population, they were becoming harder to track down and surround, requiring the deployment of still greater numbers of British troops against them. The economic cost of holding Ireland in subjection was spiraling upwards steeply, while the British economy was heading straight into a post-war slump.

99

1920

100

99. Houses in Balbriggan, County Dublin, destroyed by RIC Auxilliaries and Black and Tans on the night of 20 September 1920. In response to the operations of the guerrilla fighters of the IRA, the RIC Auxilliaries and the Black and Tans had begun, with the connivance of Dublin Castle authorities, to make indiscriminate reprisals, by burning and looting sections of towns and villages in districts where the Crown Forces had come under attack, an assignment which the regular police and the regular troops and their officers objected to taking. The Auxilliaries were also given the special task of undermining the Irish economy by destroying industries, such as creameries like the Condensed Milk Company of Ireland at Mallow, actually owned by the Unionist Sir Thomas Cleeves, bicycle factories and the Smyth's Hosiery factory at Balbriggan. At the town of Balbriggan the destruction did not stop at the hosiery factory, and a number of cottages belonging to poor people were also demolished in a completely indiscriminate way.

100. Refugees leaving the town of Balbriggan after the burning of their homes by the RIC Auxilliaries and the Black and Tans.

101

101. The Lord Mayor of Dublin receives the representatives of the American White Cross Mission to Ireland at the Mansion House, Dublin. The news from Ireland had become so black that a considerable number of prominent Americans, some, but by no means all, with Irish affiliations, formed an association called the American Commission of Inquiry into Conditions in Ireland, with the purpose of finding out just what was going on. From their investigations it was seen that a large number of people were being systematically reduced to destitution as a means of applying political and economic pressure which, it was hoped by the Lloyd George administration, would break the resistance to British rule. As a result of these findings, the American White Cross conducted an exceedingly effective world-wide fund-raising campaign and sent a delegation to Ireland to see how all those who had been reduced to penury, irrespective of their political affiliations, might be given emergency aid. This aid, although it could only offer the most minimal assistance to each individual, was instrumental in helping the struggle for Irish national independence and has, to this day, never been forgotten by the Irish people.

102

103

102. At the entrance to Brixton Prison, London, stand (*left to right*): W. Hagerty, Lord Mayor's Secretary; F.W. MacCarthy, Cork Town Clerk; and D.J. Galvin, Cork City Solicitor, attending the inquest into the death of the Lord Mayor, Terence MacSwiney, who died on hunger-strike on 25 October 1920. MacSwiney had been elected to succeed the assassinated Thomas MacCurtain as Lord Mayor of Cork. He was arrested in a raid on the city hall while presiding at a Brigade meeting of the IRA, and together with the ten men arrested at the same time, decided to go on hunger-strike in protest at the continuing arrest of public officials. Three days after the protest at Cork Gaol had begun, MacSwiney was put aboard a destroyer, deported to England and imprisoned in Brixton Gaol, where he died on 25 October 1920, on the 74th day of his refusal of food. His struggle had aroused sympathy all over Europe and America and served to publicize the Irish fight for independence more poigniantly than the fate of any other individual.

103. Terence MacSwiney's coffin aboard the Cork harbour tug *Mary Tavy* surrounded by RIC Auxilliaries and Black and Tans. A hugely attended Requiem Mass had taken place in London, after which his coffin, in the custody of his wife, sister and other immediate family relatives, was put on board the Irish Mail train at Euston to bring it, via the mail-boat to Dublin, where it was to lie in state, before being brought to Cork for interment. At Holyhead the coffin was forcibly removed from the relatives by British troops and put aboard a destroyer which sailed at once for Cork harbour, where it was trans-shipped to the tug *Mary Tavy*. The coffin was brought into the centre of the city before being handed over again. Clearly this action was taken by the British authorities in order to minimize the mass psychological effect of his obsequies, not only in Ireland but throughout all those other countries where his fate had drawn sympathetic attention.

104. Mrs Muriel MacSwiney, *née* Murphy, widow of the Lord Mayor of Cork. The crude attempts to minimize the impact of MacSwiney's death were counter-productive, particularly in the United States, where special commemorative ceremonies took place, attended by his widow, his sister Mary and other relatives.

104

105

105. Brigadier General Crozier (*centre*) with a group of RIC officers, an RIC Auxilliary officer and Black and Tans at Beggars Bush Barracks, Dublin 1920. Crozier, a regular British Army general, had been sent to Ireland six months previously to take command of the RIC Auxilliaries and the Auxilliary Cadets (Black and Tans). Finding that large numbers of them had become undisciplined and uncontrollable he began to dismiss the transgressors, but after a considerable number had been, as he thought, dismissed from the service, he found that his orders were being circumvented and overridden by civil servants in the administration, so that the dismissals were not taking place. The Auxilliaries were sent a clear signal that they were above the law and that no notice would be taken of their conduct, no matter how criminal, and that even murder would be condoned, as in the case of Canon Magner, parish priest of Dunmanway and Father Griffen of Galway and many ordinary citizens with no political orientation, including women and children. Such a situation was so utterly repugnant to Crozier that he tendered his resignation and, as he did not hide his reasons for it, severely damaged the image created by Lloyd George's boast that 'We have murder by the throat'. His 'police action' had come to have the bitterness of a civil war.

106

106. Some of the members of Michael Collins's Active Service Unit. On the morning of 21 November, a group of Collins' counter-intelligence men shot dead some 14 British special agents belonging to a group, according to General Crozier, that was set up by Sir Henry Wilson to carry out assassinations in Ireland early in 1920. This pre-emptive strike by Collins led to reprisals; a crowd of spectators at a Gaelic football match at Croke Park were machine-gunned that afternoon by Black and Tans, several of the spectators were killed and a considerable number wounded. Until now the soldiers of the IRA had been unpaid volunteers who provided their services in their free time while continuing to work in their everyday avocations. As the end of 1920 approached, Michael Collins became convinced that the worsening conditions in Dublin required a special corps that would be full-time paid soldiers of the Republic. Choosing from the Dublin Brigade he established a body of 50 men who resigned their employment and received £4 10s a day.

107

107. Union officals under arrest outside the head office of the Irish Transport and General Workers Union: (*left to right*) Thomas Johnson, William O'Brien, Thomas Foran and Seamas Hughes). The emergency powers were now being applied in Ireland against the Trades Union movement. Earlier in 1920, the Union official William O'Brien had been arrested in Dublin, deported to London and imprisoned in Wormwood Scrubbs without any charge. He went on hunger-strike until his release; Cathal O'Shannon had a similar experience. Ever since 1913, the Irish Transport and General Workers Union had come under the suspicious scrutiny of the British authorities and after 'Bloody Sunday', a particularly disruptive raid was made on Liberty Hall by RIC Auxilliaries and Black and Tans. The Crown Forces stormed the building with drawn revolvers, removed and destroyed records, burning some in the street outside and arrested some 24 union staff, a number of women among them.

108. British troops erecting barricades of barbed wire to prevent access to Dublin City Hall. In the last weeks of 1920 the Crown Forces began preparations for a reign of terror that could under no circumstances be called a 'police action'. In Cork, on the night of 11 December, Auxilliaries sealed off a large part of the centre of the city before the hour of curfew, driving everyone out at gun-point, then large numbers of Auxilliaries and Black and Tans doused buildings with petrol and ignited them. That night over £2 million pounds worth (as valued in 1920) of indiscriminate damage was done. British insurance companies refused to pay compensation on the subsequent claims. Nothing of this magnitude of civic destruction was known in Europe again until the Nazi's *Kristalnacht*.

108

109

109. Inside the armoured gate of Dublin Castle. Lloyd George could no longer make any pretence of pursuing a 'police action'. Ireland was an occupied country undergoing a guerrilla war for liberation and within it, the British organs of administration were under siege and disintegrating. However, a further period of frightfulness was about to begin.

110. Passers-by stop to read a proclamation relating to extensions of the death penalty in the areas of Ireland now under Martial Law in December 1920. Although most of Ireland was now under Martial Law, Lloyd George refused, publicly, to admit that a state of war existed, worried at the effect that such an admission would have on world opinion as well as on the domestic population of England. For more than three years, protest had been growing in England at the methods which were being employed in Ireland, The protest was led, at first, by famous writers such as H.G. Wells and George Bernard Shaw, and by the British Labour Party which showed its solidarity with its fraternal party in Ireland in every way that it could. It had become plain to the British government that a merely verbal propaganda war would not suffice and steps were put in hand to fill this gap.

110

111

111. A fake-actuality photograph purporting to show Royal Irish Constabulary Auxilliaries engaging the IRA in County Kerry. The desperation of the instigators of Lloyd George's policy in Ireland, faced with the growing public reaction of ordinary people in England, Scotland and Wales is demonstrated by the fact that, in mid-January 1921, a couple of film camera operators called Gemmell and Starmer were sent over to make fake newsreels which would show how the Auxilliaries were getting on top of the situation, militarily speaking. One of these supposed coverages showed Auxilliaries allegedly fighting with and capturing an IRA party in County Kerry. This still photograph was taken at the same time. These films and photographs were for circulation in England only and no great care was shown in selecting their locations, for, apart from a few scenes shot near the British Army artillery range in the Glen of Imaal in County Wicklow, the venues were all in County Dublin. However, the footage found its way to Ireland where it was greeted with derision by audiences. This particular engagement, though supposedly Kerry, was in fact shot on the Vico Road, Killiney.

112. The Dublin Custom House burns. There is nothing fake about this photograph however. All the taxation administration and all the local government administration for Ireland was controlled from offices in the Dublin Custom House, where the master files were held. Just before 1 pm on 25 May, the Dublin Brigade of the IRA made a lightning attack on the Custom House, forcing their way in and making the staff evacuate the building, all of whom complied except the caretaker who resisted and was shot. Before Crown Forces could respond, the building was ablaze and the fire stations having been held up simultaneously, the fire took a firm hold. Before they could disperse, the raiding party was engaged by regular troops and Auxilliaries; a number of the raiders were shot dead and some 80 of them captured. The destruction of Gandon's beautiful building had been reluctantly undertaken after much discussion between Michael Collins and the IRA staff, but a severely disorganizing blow had been struck at the heart of the British administration in Ireland.

112

113. British regular troops in Beresford Place guard suspects while they are searched by RIC Auxilliaries.

114. The body of one of the IRA Custom House raiding party lies in the roadway just outside Liberty Hall in Beresford Place. Beside the body stands a British Army Medical Corps orderly and in the background British regular troops mount guard with fixed bayonets.

113

114

116

115. British troops search for documents in the debris of the Dublin Custom House. The information destroyed by the IRA raid could not be replaced by the British authorities; also much documentation of historical interest was lost, but worse losses were to come.

116. James Talbot, Viscount Fitzalan and Viscountess Fitzalan. He was to be the last Lieutenant General and General Governor of Ireland. The Better Government of Ireland Act, which gave *de juri* status to the *de facto* partitioning of Ireland, came into force on 3 May 1921 and Lord Fitzalan came into office on 19 May, the same day that the election for the Parliament of Southern Ireland was to take place. That for the Parliament of Northern Ireland was to be held on 24 May. Lord Fitzalan issued the proclamation summoning both parliaments to meet in June. The Republican Government in Dublin declared that this would be regarded as an election for the Second Dail. In Southern Ireland the election resulted in all but four of the 133 seats being filled by candidates with Republican sympathies; the only opposition seats were four Unionist candidates returned by Trinity College Dublin, among them, Sir James Craig.

117. The first session of the Northern Parliament on 7 June was held in the Council Chamber of Belfast City Hall, the first venue for such meetings until the completion of the Parliament House at Stormont. As the Republican candidates returned had pledged to attend the Second Dail in Dublin, none was present here. The Irish Parliamentary Party candidates who had been returned did not, at first, take their seats although they were to do so later. With the formal establishment of this regional legislature, the Unionist Party reorganized itself, becoming the Ulster Unionist Party which was to hold power in Northern Ireland for 51 years.

118. This photograph, taken after the first meeting of the Northern Parliament (*above*), shows the character of the right-wing, oligarchic Conservative political structure that was helped into power in Northern Ireland by the Tory establishment in England. The chief supporters of this new regime were (*left to right*) the Marquis of Londonderry, Lady Craig, Captain Herbert Dixon, Lord Pirrie, Lady Pirrie and Sir James Craig. Only Sir Edward Carson and Sir Henry Wilson were absent, the latter because he expected to be ordering troops into Southern Ireland.

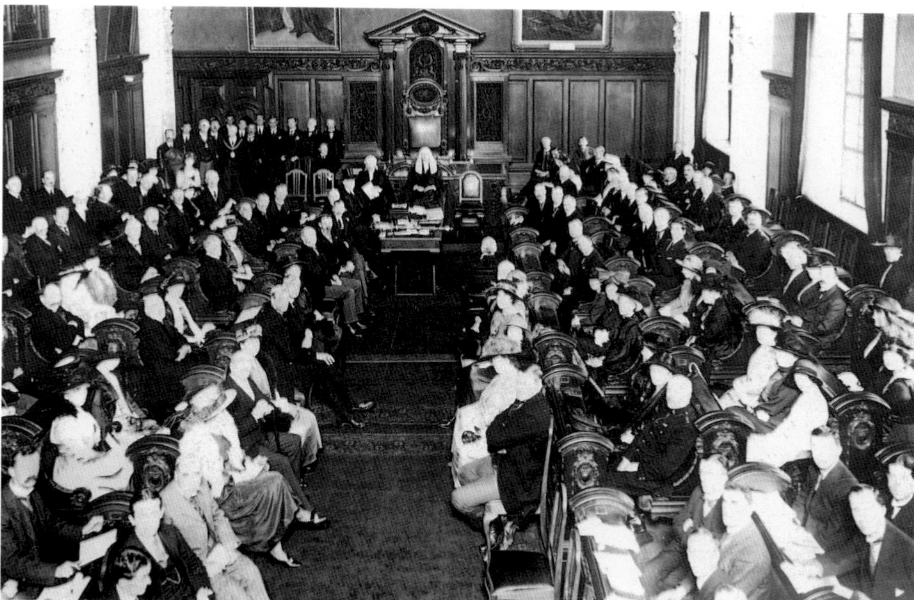
117

118

119

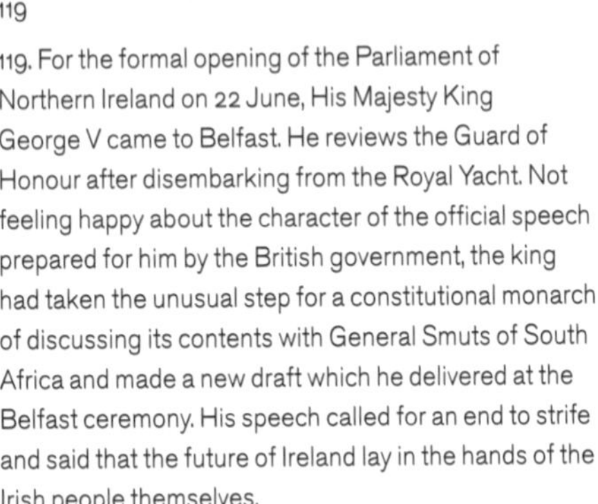

119. For the formal opening of the Parliament of Northern Ireland on 22 June, His Majesty King George V came to Belfast. He reviews the Guard of Honour after disembarking from the Royal Yacht. Not feeling happy about the character of the official speech prepared for him by the British government, the king had taken the unusual step for a constitutional monarch of discussing its contents with General Smuts of South Africa and made a new draft which he delivered at the Belfast ceremony. His speech called for an end to strife and said that the future of Ireland lay in the hands of the Irish people themselves.

120. The crowd outside the Mansion House, Dublin. King George's speech had thrown the government at Westminster into confusion and another event seemed about to wreck any chance of peace. On the afternoon of the king's speech, the president of Sinn Fein, de Valera was captured in a raid on his secret headquarters. This was a blow for all in the British administration who felt that now was the moment to try for a peaceful settlement. Against opposition from the faction that was seeking all-out war, A.W. Cope, the Under Secretary for Ireland, who favoured negotiations, managed to secure de Valera's release the next day. Two days later de Valera received a letter from Lloyd George inviting him to discussions in London with Sir James Craig. After consultation with the Dail cabinet and Southern Unionists, he said that talks could not begin until hostilities had ceased. Although the proposal was resisted by the British government, Southern Unionist Viscount Middleton was instrumental in persuading Lloyd George to agree to a truce, which came into force on 11 July.

121. Arthur Griffith arrives at the Mansion House, Dublin, after his release from Mountjoy Prison, to attend the inaugural meeting of the second Dail on 16 August 1921. The first of the Dail members to be released, he was followed by Robert Barton, Eoin MacNeill, Eamon Duggan and Michael Staines. However, 34 members of the Dail still remained in prison.

122. Harry Boland and Michael Collins at a hurling match at Croke Park, August 1921. Everywhere in the South of Ireland the truce was greeted with great relief, as it was by Nationalists in the North. It seemed the days of savage guerrilla warfare were over and many believed that the struggle for national independence had been won, an illusion which gradually evaporated.

120

121

122

124

123. De Valera enters No. 10 Downing Street, the British Prime Minister's official residence in London, 14 July. With the Anglo-Irish truce successfully in operation, de Valera agreed to meet Lloyd George and left for London with his chief advisers, Robert Barton, Erskine Childers, Arthur Griffith, Count Plunkett and Austin Stack. But agreement as to the terms of a settlement could not be reached; de Valera made it plain that the terms proposed by the British administration were not likely to be accepted by the forthcoming meeting of the Second Dail, and so it proved. Two months of negotiations by correspondence ensued before another meeting was to be effected and in those two months of truce, the relentless pressure of the military, the RIC Auxilliaries and the Black and Tans was suspended, though their presence in Ireland continued. But something which had not occurred throughout all the years of fighting took place – the unity of Sinn Fein began to disintegrate.

124. Four of the delegates (and their clerical staff), appointed from the Republican side aboard the mail-boat at Holyhead on their way to London to resume negotiations: (*left to right*) Arthur Griffith, Edmund Duggan, Robert Barton and George Gavan Duffy. Michael Collins is not among them, since he travelled to London on the following day. De Valera is also not to be seen, for it had been arranged that he would remain in Dublin. A further difference was that the delegates, on Lloyd George's insistence, had been empowered to be Ministers Plenipotentiary, a further psychological strain imposed upon men who, although of unimpeachable probity, were not professional diplomats, a situation which the British premier was to exploit powerfully to ensure that the negotiations took the direction that he wished them to take. Against them, in the British cabinet room was to be arrayed an exceptionally able group of highly experienced politicians of long standing, including Lord Birkenhead (F.E. Smith), Winston Churchill, Austin Chamberlain, the Secretary of State for War Sir L. Worthington Evans and the Chief Secretary for Ireland Sir Hamar Greenwood, a formidable team lead by the 'Welsh Wizard' himself.

After four years of a guerrilla war of steadily increasing intensity, the sudden cessation of conflict comes as almost as great a mass-psychological shock as the opening of hostilities, but a truce is not peace. The tension and insecurity of war continue while the outcome remains unknown and both sides try to consolidate their positions in the event that no accommodation may result and warfare may be resumed. Such stress is more acutely felt by the weaker power and it is the negotiators of that power who are always placed under the greatest strain, while the more powerful side invariably seeks to take advantage of this very fact. With many years of special training behind them, diplomats are in a far better position to cope with these pressures, but it is hard indeed for the inexperienced to undertake this very exacting duty with the same proficiency and detachment that is possible for the professionals. Painfully aware of what the Irish people had endured and equally filled with hope for what might be achieved, the Sinn Fein negotiators found themselves torn apart intellectually and emotionally and the same effect was felt within the Sinn Fein Party as a whole. In the face of this intense dichotomy, the unity of Sinn Fein was to crumble for the first time and the cleft was to widen into Civil War.

125. Three of the delegates at Hans Place, London, 10 October 1921 (*left to right*) George Gavan Duffy, Michael Collins and Arthur Griffith.

A country divided

Trying for a Treaty

132. The sharp division in Irish public opinion veering between jubilation and consternation was quickly reflected in the Dail speeches which commenced its debate on the issue. It met on 14 December, not in the round room of the Mansion House, but in the Convocation Hall of the National University of Ireland in Earlsfort Terrace. The first day of the debate was almost exclusively occupied with deciding whether the delegates had the right to sign without the consent of the cabinet in Dublin. As plenipotentiaries they did have the right to do so, although some held that this meant the delegates had broken their oath to defend the Republic. This most unhappy situation led to increasing acrimony and bitter division as the debate continued, particularly as it became clear that the Free State, as the 26 Counties area was to be called, would not even get full Dominion status.

132

133

133. In order to promote a reaction favourable to the Treaty, the British government instigated the release of certain Irish political prisoners with great rapidity. Here some are seen leaving Kilmainham Gaol, Dublin, in mid-December. Many of those, however, who had been tried and convicted under the Defence of the Realm Act directives and other emergency legislation, were not released for some months.

134. Following immediately on the release of the prisoners from Kilmainham, the British authorities evacuated the gaol itself. They were probably glad to be able to do so, since it was here at Kilmainham that the leaders of the 1916 Rising had been shot. However, only a short period of six months was to pass before Kilmainham Goal was once again crowded with political prisoners.

134

135

135. De Valera and some of his supporters on the steps of the National University building, 10 January 1922. Because he felt that the Republican position had been compromised, Eamon de Valera had resigned as president the previous day. On that same day, a motion was put before the Dail 'that Mr de Valera be re-elected President of the Irish Republic'. This motion was lost by only two votes. On the following day Arthur Griffith was proposed as President of the Dail. While the vote for this motion was taking place, de Valera and all the Republican supporters left the Chamber and are seen here on the steps of the National University building. On the left at the top, with dark hair is Sean O'Mahony who had been returned as a Republican TD for Enniskillen (in the North of Ireland); immediately below and to his left is Robert Barton TD. Standing in the foreground, hat in hand, is Cathal Brugha TD, who had been Minister for Defence; on his left hand is Mrs Pearse TD, mother of Padraic Pearse; and on her left, de Valera. Standing behind Cathal Brugha is Sean McEntee TD. A tragic sense of loss is seen on all their faces as they anticipate the unhappiness to come.

136. Among the Republicans who left the chamber was the Secretary of Sinn Fein, Austin Stack TD from Kerry. His health had been severely damaged through his participation in a number of hunger-strikes and was to be broken completely by his sufferings during the coming Civil War. Behind his right shoulder stands Mrs Tom Clarke.

136

137

138

137. Arthur Griffith at the meeting held on 14 January 1922, of pro-Treaty TDs summoned by him to act as 'the Parliament of Southern Ireland', to put into effect the provisions of the Articles of Agreement for the Treaty by electing a provisional government for Southern Ireland. No TD who sat in the Dail solely for a constituency now in Northern Ireland was summoned to this meeting, nor did any of the Republican TDs attend. Curiously enough, this meeting was not summoned by Lord Fitzalan, the Governor General and representative of King George V, who had summoned the previous abortive gathering of that name, but by Arthur Griffith who signed the summons in his capacity as chairman of the Irish delegation of plenipotentiaries, a singular action, as the body referred to had been nominated to negotiate the terms of an agreement, not to put the agreed terms into effect. Weird things were happening in relation to constitutional matters and political allegiances were changing overnight.

138. Michael Collins attended the same meeting. The gathering consisted of 60 pro-Treaty members of the Dail and the three Unionist members elected by Trinity College Dublin; the fourth Unionist member so elected, Sir James Craig, did not attend. He was later to take his seat and vote in the Dail under curious circumstances (*see page 269*). In pursuance of the conditions of the Agreement, this body elected a Provisional Government of Southern Ireland and elected Michael Collin as chairman. The intricacies of the change in the balance of power and their implications seem reflected in the serious and thoughtful expression which has replaced the smile with which this motion-picture scene began. A completely new power structure had been revealed.

139. Two days later, on 16 January 1922, Lord Fitzalan received the cabinet of the Provisional Government at Dublin Castle, handing over power to them in the name of the British government and took his leave. The first Governor General of the Irish Free State was not appointed until 6 December 1922. Here members of the Provisional Government Kevin O'Higgins, Michael Collins and Eamon Duggan, are seen leaving the castle after the ceremony.

139

140

140. In the twinkling of an eye, the unarmed Republican Police had been replaced by a new body, the Civic Guard; the first contingent is seen on 17 January, the day after the handover of Dublin Castle, marching in to take up their duties. Following the precedent of the Republican Police, this body was also to be unarmed, as our Garda Siochána (police) is to this day.

141. With the departure of Lord Fitzalan from the Vice-Regal Lodge in Phoenix Park on 17 January 1922, the guard was changed there for the last time and left, while everywhere in Ireland, except for three port garrisons, British troops began preparations to leave. The hated RIC Auxilliaries and the Black and Tans had already done so.

141

142. In the old Royal Irish Constabulary Depot in Phoenix Park, new recruits for the Civic Guard beginning their training in January 1922. Due to the deliberate destruction of the Irish economy over the previous four years, and the general post-war slump as well as the release of internees and political prisoners, together with demobilization from the British Army, there was a very high level of chronic unemployment in Ireland. As a result, the Free State government appeal for recruits to the Civic Guard and to the Army met with a wide positive response.

143. General Richard Mulcahy (*centre in civilian clothes*) appointed Minister for Defence by the Provisional Government, with Mr Ernest Blythe, the newly appointed Minister for Trade and Commerce (*on Mulcahy's left*) on 18 January 1922. Michael Collins was now leading the Provisional Government of the Irish Free State in the direction favoured by the IRB. New men were coming into political prominence. Under the terms of the Articles of Agreement, a general election had to be held within three months to establish a permanent Free State Government.

144. At the end of January, a contingent of the newly formed Free State National Army took over Beggars Bush Barracks, Dublin, which had been evacuated by the RIC Auxilliaries. General Eoin O'Duffy, the Chief of Staff (*in civilian clothes*), looked on while the Minister for Defence, General Mulcahy (*in uniform*), addressed the troops, telling them that they were 'going ahead under the old flag with the old aspirations in their hearts, still guarding the old ideals'. The buttons of their uniforms were careful replicas of those worn by the Irish Volunteers in the 1916 Rising. But as more and more of the formerly British Barracks were handed over to Free State troops, the brigades of the IRA began to split up into pro-Treaty and anti-Treaty brigades and the anti-Treaty groups began to pre-empt the handovers by occupying empty barracks themselves and, where this was not possible, other buildings. A very ominous disintegration and reorientation were taking place inside the IRA itself, which were causing grave concern to a great many political bodies and organizations, and would soon to lead to actual fighting.

143

1922

144

145

145. On 12 February, de Valera, who was still the president of Sinn Fein, opened his campaign against the treaty in favour of his alternative plan, known as 'Document No. 2'. This plan allowed for a form of external relationship with the British Commonwealth but which would not have required the swearing of an oath of allegiance to the British Crown; rather resembling, in fact, that which eventually transpired in 1938 under the name of Éire.

146. The crowd in O'Connell Street listens to de Valera's speech. It is very hard for us, today, to realize the acute disappointment felt by the great numbers of ordinary people, who having sacrificed so much in the five years of bitter struggle for the Republic, saw that Republican ideal they had cherished for over a century, snatched away at the very last moment and replaced with a settlement that required allegiance to the Crown with less than Dominion status for the new state.

146

147. The first British armoured car to be handed over to the Free State Army was this Rolls-Royce 'Whippet', with its commander, Captain Bill Stapleton, holding the flag at Strand Barracks, Limerick. The most effective type of armoured vehicle to have been used in Ireland, the 'Whippets' were to form the main mobile armour of the Free State Army. The armoured rotating turret carried a water-cooled Vickers machine-gun capable of sustaining longer bursts of firing than the Hotchkiss without overheating. It was realized that trouble was brewing in Limerick and this car was sent down from the Free State-held Portobello Barracks in Dublin for reconnaissance work in the troubled area under the command of Captain Bill Stapleton, with a crew of four – two Free State officers and two Black and Tans who had been seconded to train the Free State officers on how to handle the vehicle. On the completion of their training mission, while on their way back to Dublin, the crew stopped at Templemore Barracks, being unaware that the troops there had changed over to the Republican side. All five of the men were arrested and soon afterwards the car was handed over to Commandant Ernie O'Malley of the Limerick Brigade of the IRA, who had also gone over to the Republican side.

147

1922

148. By February 1922, the pivotal importance of Limerick City on the Shannon was appreciated by both the Free State and Republican sides. Whoever controlled Limerick also controlled the Shannon bridges commanding the South and West. On 23 February, the British were due to evacuate Limerick barracks. A fews days before this, the Limerick Brigade of the IRA declared for the Republican side. When the British troops pulled out, they handing the barracks to pro-Treaty troops of the First Western Division, under officers from Dublin, drawn mainly from members of Michael Collins's intelligence corps. Commandant Ernie O'Malley of the Mid Limerick Brigade of the IRA sent for 70 men from the Second Southern Division in Tipperary, hoping to be able to capture the Strand Barracks and King John's Castle with this augmented force. This plan miscarried, and his Republican force occupied a number of hotels in the city. O'Malley made the Glentworth Hotel his headquarters; the main entrance is seen here guarded by Second Southern Division men. Civil war seemed almost certain for a few days, but eventually a compromise was reached.

149

149. General Eoin O'Duffy, Chief of Staff of the Free State Army, wearing the shamrock on St Patrick's Day, 1922. This is one of the earliest photographs to show him in Free State Army uniform. It was taken at Beggars Bush Barracks, Dublin, where the Provisional Government of the Irish Free State had first established its general headquarters.

150. Ladies decorating Free State Army soldiers with bunches of shamrock at the GHQ, Beggars Bush, Dublin on St Patrick's Day. Note that a notice displaying the initials RAMC (Royal Army Medical Corps) has not yet been removed.

150

151

151. Michael Collins's great meeting in College Green on 20 April, drew an even larger crowd than did that of de Valera in March. The huge crowd came to hear Michael Collins's view of the Articles of Agreement.

152. Michael Collins awaits his turn to speak.

153. Michael Collins speaking. He urged his listeners to accept the terms of the Agreement as a step towards freedom and independence, giving the 'freedom to get freedom' and assured them that the Boundary Commission would award large areas of Northern Ireland to the Irish Free State on the basis of demographic statistics.

153

152

154

154. General Sean MacKeon inspects his troops after the take-over of Athlone Barracks in the name of the Provisional Government on 31 March 1922. Marching behind him, to his left, is Colonel A.T. Lawlor, who gave the Free State troops their first instruction in handling field-guns. He was, in retirement, many years later, to head the Maritime Institute of Ireland.

155. General MacKeon addresses his troops and members of the public after the take-over. Known as 'the Blacksmith of Ballinalee' for his exploits during the guerrilla war against the Crown Forces, he was among the first outstanding commanders to become persuaded of the necessity of taking the pro-Treaty side. He was also convinced that an Irish Army should be subject to a civilian government and that the IRA Executive had become a military junta. An exceptionally able commander, he had long established a tradition of humanity to his prisoners which was to be continued during his service throughout the Civil War.

155

156

156. Armed anti-Treaty members of the IRA march down Grafton Street, Dublin. The Dublin Brigade of the IRA took the Republican side in the power struggle now going on and, armed with rifles puchased in Germany, and landed at Helvick on 2 March, it began to secure bases for itself in Dublin, since it was now abundantly clear to the Republican groups in the IRA that the Provisional Government was doing its utmost to ensure that the barracks evacuated by British troops were handed over to Free State troops only. Both the pro-Treaty and the Republican factions of the IRA had sought to hold an Army convention at which both sides would be represented, but this had been forbidden by Michael Collins's cabinet, so the Republican faction finally summoned an Army convention unilaterally for 26 March 1922.

157

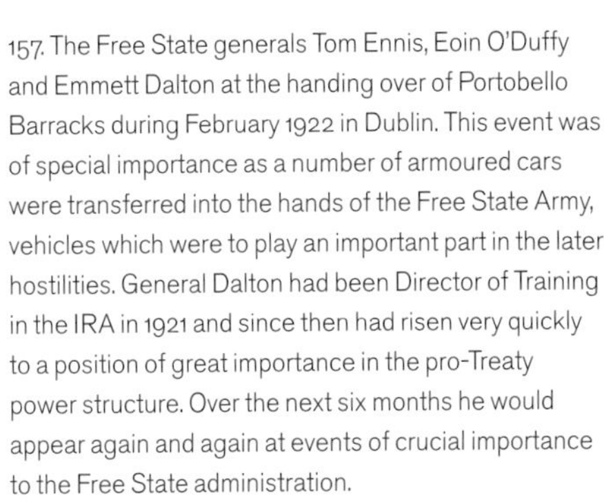

157. The Free State generals Tom Ennis, Eoin O'Duffy and Emmett Dalton at the handing over of Portobello Barracks during February 1922 in Dublin. This event was of special importance as a number of armoured cars were transferred into the hands of the Free State Army, vehicles which were to play an important part in the later hostilities. General Dalton had been Director of Training in the IRA in 1921 and since then had risen very quickly to a position of great importance in the pro-Treaty power structure. Over the next six months he would appear again and again at events of crucial importance to the Free State administration.

158. General Sean MacKeon (*centre*), and on his left, the Republican Commandant Dan Breen leave the Mansion House at the Sinn Fein Party conference of 22 February. In the midst of the widening divisions, the 3,000 delegates of the conference agreed to a proposal that the convention stand adjourned for three months until the constitution of the Irish Free State be laid before it and voted on in full session. This was to be one of the last major peace moves to be agreed by any large gathering.

158

1922

159. The ruins of the *Freeman's Journal* printing presses. On 29 March, three days after the Republican Army convention took place, the *Freeman's Journal* presses were destroyed by order of the Executive of the Republican IRA, who claimed that a false and scurillous account of the proceedings of the Republican Army Convention had been given in the newspaper. The most serious aspect of this event was not the loss of the presses, but of the very large collection of photographic plates held by the *Freeman's Journal* which had been the first Irish newspaper to use photographs, and had been doing so daily from the 1890s onwards. It proved an incalculable loss to the visual documentation of Irish life. On the same day, the Republicans mounted a brilliantly planned operation whereby they captured a British transport vessel, the SS *Upnor* at Cobh, in Cork Harbour. She was loaded with rifles, mines and other munitions from evacuated barracks and the capture of these undoubtedly led to a prolonging of the course of the Civil War, without in any way determining its eventual outcome.

159

160

160. Republicans in County Mayo attend a commemoration of fallen comrades. To Republicans everywhere in Ireland, the actions of the Provisional Government now appeared as a betrayal of all those comrades who had fallen from Easter week onwards and of all those who had sacrificed their economic livelihoods and their careers to the selfless upholding of the Republican ideal. As they commemorated their dead they vowed that they would not be entrapped in what seemed to them to be the snare of the 'Free State'.

161. A riot in a Belfast street.The month of March saw the enactment by the Northern Government of a draconian measure, the Special Powers Bill. Under this bill, Coroners' Courts could be dispensed with and inquests forbidden, trial by jury suspended, new and savage penalties introduced as well as an extension to the infliction of the death penalty. These measures were in the main directed against Nationalists and Roman Catholics in possession of arms, while at the same time licences for guns were to be readily given to Orangemen and Unionists. A special armed, part-time branch of the police force, the B-Specials was established and within a very short while 'ethnic cleansing' was being conducted every night, with dozens of deaths every month. The response of the British government to this was not to use the very large number of British troops stationed there to intervene, but to supply further funding for arms at the request of Sir James Craig. Michael Collins's attempt to stop the progroms was to be a complete failure.

161

162

1922

162. This militaristic build-up in both North and South was not lost on children, as these Dublin boys show. Such indoctrination became a regular part of the culture of Irish childhood during this period.

163. Sir Edward Carson and Sir James Craig. Michael Collins had several meetings with Sir James Craig, first to try to persuade him to bring the anti-Nationalist and anti-Catholic pogroms to an end, and then to seek a more ethnically balanced adjustment of the border between the two countries. While he was met with a promise in regard to the pogroms, which nevertheless continued, he met with utter failure with regard to the border question. That was to be left to a Boundary Commission for final settlement.

163

165

164. In the Free State, training of unarmed Civic Guard at Phoenix Park, Dublin, continued during April. The fact that the Free State government was determined to follow the precedent set by the unarmed status of the Republican police seems to have been one of the few hopeful signs in the steadily deteriorating situation in both the North and South of Ireland at this time.

165. Commandant Rory O'Connor after the eventual meeting, on 9 April, of the postponed Irish Republican Army Convention. At this meeting a motion proposing the immediate setting up of a military dictatorship was lost by only two votes, one of them Cathal Brugha's. Instead, a Republican Executive and a Republican Army Council were formed. The eventuality, foreseen by Sean MacKeon, of the formation of a military junta, had drawn closer. The South of Ireland was one very fatal step nearer to Civil War. If Collins was indeed correct in holding an informed view that the Irish Republican Army could not hold out against another onslaught from the British, he failed to convince the leaders of the Republican Army. Could this failure be in part due to the information and assessments provided by Collins's immensely efficient intelligence network being kept too confidential and not being disclosed widely enough in time? Had such a policy of disclosure to the leaders of the IRA been brought into operation in January and February, might not the danger of eventual Civil War have been reduced? Cathal Brugha's rejection of the notion of forming a military junta suggests that his mind was not as closed as has often been suggested, and that as Minister for Defence in the Second Dail, he could have been open to persuasion if really convincing evidence had been placed before him in time. Collins's involvement with secrecy and secret organizations rendered him a bad communicator.

164

166. The Four Courts, Dublin, 15 April. Once formed, the Executive of the IRA lost no time in issuing orders for certain buildings in Dublin to be occupied, notably the Four Courts, Kilmainham Gaol and a range of buildings along the east side of O'Connell Street which was to become known as 'the Block'. The Four Courts, seen here on the morning after the occupation, was to be made the Republican headquarters and raids were made on Free State government stores and requisitions made to provision it. Cut off from funding from the financial resources of the Dail, the Republicans were unable to pay tradesmen for goods and services, so began to raid and seize Free State funds held in banks, and requisition cars, lorries and petrol.

166

167. Free State Army troops occupying Sligo Town Hall, 16 April. The Free State Agreement Act had been passed and had received Royal Assent. The bill required that a general election take place in the Free State before 30 June. The Free State faction, the Republican faction and the Irish Labour Party began hurriedly preparing their election plans and election meetings were held all over the South of Ireland. Only those of the Irish Labour Party were free from interference by the opposing sides. In Sligo town, a meeting to be addressed by Arthur Griffith and other pro-Treaty politicians on Sunday 16 April was threatened by IRA troops; as a result Free State Army troops were brought in to protect it.

168

168. Republican troops with rifles on a lorry, Sligo town on Sunday 16 April, seeking to prevent Free State politicians from holding a pro-Treaty meeting.

169

169. A group of Free State supporters including Darryl Figgis, at the extreme right with beard, in Sligo. Only the deployment of a strong body of Free State troops under General Sean MacKeon enabled this meeting to take place. Five days before this tension-dominated meeting, the Irish Labour Party had denounced the forceful disruption of election meetings and stated in a manifesto 'The Labour Movement resolutely opposes, and will use all its powers against any body of men, official or unofficial, regular forces or irregular forces, who seek to impose their will upon the people by virtue of their armaments alone.' On 26 April, the Labour Party sought to bring about a meeting between the leaders of the Provisional Government and of the Republicans, but this peace plan was rejected both by Michael Collins and Arthur Griffith.

170

171

170. Army commanders from both sides at the Dublin Mansion House on 8 May 1922. During the first week in May, actual fighting with casualties had broken out in Kilkenny. So critical was the situation that a group of commanding officers from both sides arranged to meet in a desperate bid to preserve peace so that a general election could be held. This is the last photograph of the military leaders of the opposing sides together: (*left to right*) Sean MacKeon (Free State), Sean Moylan (Republican), Eoin O'Duffy (Free State), Liam Lynch (Republican), Gearoid O'Sullivan (Free State) and Liam Mellowes (Republican).

171. Republican and Free State leaders in the Dublin Mansion House garden, 20 May 1922. A momentous agreement had been reached that seemed likely to avert Civil War. The Sinn Fein Party was to put forward a panel of agreed candidates, of which 58 were to be nominated by the anti-Treaty side and 66 by the supporters of the Treaty. After the signing of this electoral pact the TDs posed for this photograph: (*front row left to right*) Constance Markievicz (Republican), Arthur Griffith (Free State), Eamon de Valera (Republican), Michael Collins (Free State) and Harry Boland (Republican). A surge of hope swept through the Free State, for the plan was to defer the final decision on the Treaty until there was time to consider the question calmly, after the Free State Constitution had been published and the election had taken place. But alarm bells started in Whitehall and during a debate in the Commons, Sir Henry Wilson said: 'If serious trouble arises on the frontier between the 6 Counties and the 26 Counties, I hope that the Government will not restrain the military from crossing the frontier in their own self-defence.' Both Arthur Griffith and Michael Collins, present in the Distinguished Strangers' Gallery, heard this speech.

172. Nominations for what came to be called the Pact Election were posted up on a pillar of the Bank of Ireland, College Green, Dublin, 27 May. The nomination forms were not issued for the Third Dail, but for the Provisional Parliament pursuant to the Free State (Agreement) Act, 1922, which required the elected candidates to take an oath of allegiance to King George. The era of exclusion of Republicans by the oath had begun.

173. Constance Markievicz, as a convinced Republican who had made her home among the poor of Dublin, must have found this election (nomination posters for which are on the wall beyond her), a distressing experience for, if elected, she did not intend to take the oath of allegiance.

172

173

174

175

174. Michael Collins's pro-Treaty meeting in Cork city on 14 June drew an immense crowd. The day before he had been in London meeting Winston Churchill because of disagreement between the Irish and the British drafters of the Treaty, no copy of which nor draft of the Constitution of the Irish Free State had been put before the electorate.

175. Collins in the course of his address. Whether because of pressure brought to bear upon him by Churchill or for whatever other reason, Collins said: '… I am not hampered now by being on a platform where there are Coalitionists, I can make a straight appeal to you – to the citizens of Cork, to vote for the candidates you think best of…' The Coalition Pact had been ripped apart by this statement, producing political turmoil just before polling day.

176. Collins's clear breach of the Election Pact so enraged some of the Republicans present that they began to fire hand-guns into the air at that public meeting; the one on the left is clearly a Mauser Parabellum, that on the right is harder to identify but may be a Browning automatic.

176

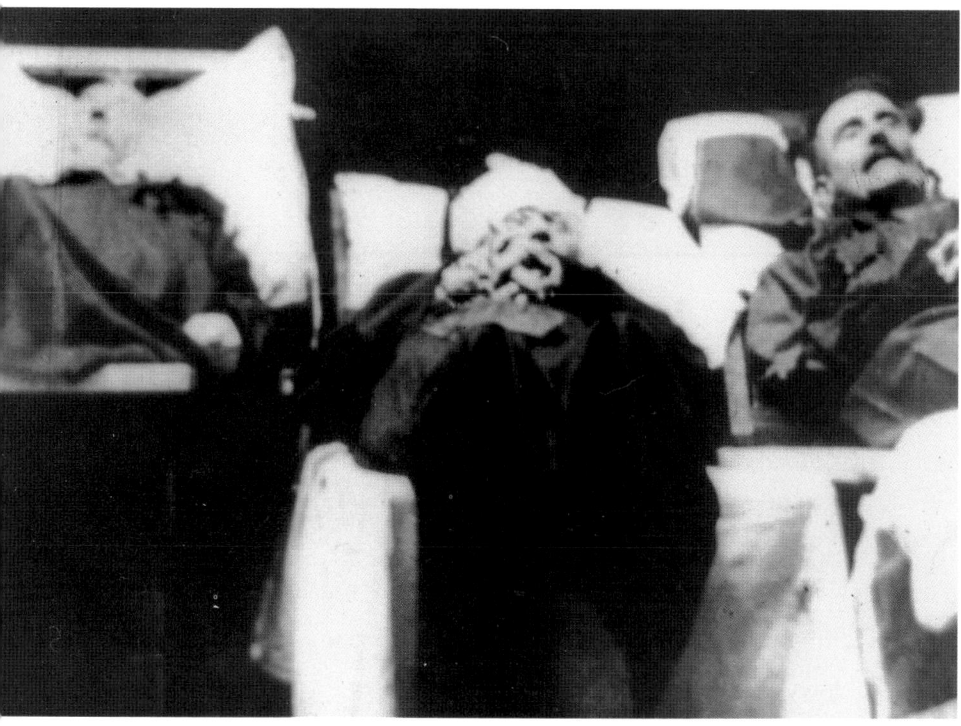

177

177. Bodies in an improvised mortuary at a Belfast hospital in June 1922. As though the tensions of the last weeks were not enough while the Pact Election was proceeding, it appeared that Sir James Craig in the North had been unable to keep his promise to Michael Collins that the pogroms would be stopped. The policy of permitting fear for their lives to induce Roman Catholics to move into what amounted to religious ghettos continued and killings increased. The shooting of two B-Specials (armed part-time RUC) in Belfast led to indiscriminate carnage and a large Catholic hospital, overcrowded with wounded, came under attack by an armed Unionist mob.

178. A murdered infant in a Belfast hospital. Community hatred in the North had reached the stage where age no longer counted and the Catholic population was faced with a terror such as even the Black and Tans and the Auxilliaries had not exceeded.

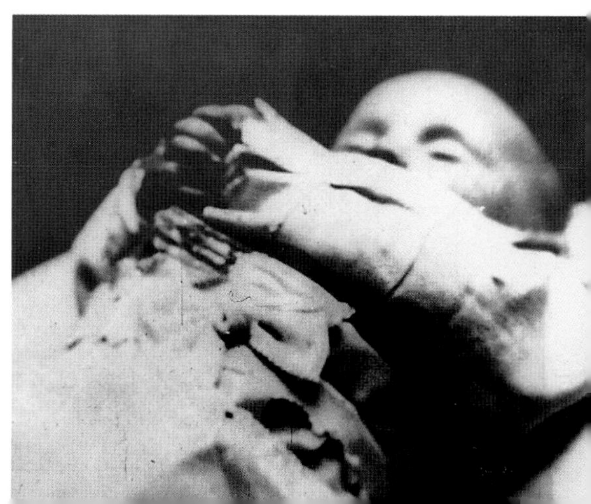

178

179

180

181

179. A refugee child from Belfast arriving in Dublin, June 1922. The tension and instability of war were everywhere in the public mind as the local authorities in the Free State, on both sides of the political divide, sought to find accommodation for the women and children arriving from the North in lorries.

180. Refugee children arriving in Dublin in June 1922, being assisted by the Free State Army. But even as these humanitarian efforts were going forward, General Macready, the commander of the British military forces still in Ireland, was moving his remaining troops to invest Dublin so that, should the election lead to the declaration of a Republic, the capital city could be seized immediately.

181. On the last day of the campaign, 15 June, Michael Collins addressed a meeting in front of O'Donovan's Hotel, Clonkility, County Cork and then went to visit the place of his birth.

182. De Valera moved through the Southern counties still adhering in his speeches to the terms of the Electoral Pact although he realized it was now a dead letter. Here he is seen making one of his last pre-election speeches at Mooncoin, County Kilkenny on 13 June.

183

1922

183. Collins stands in the ruins of his home, destroyed by the Black and Tans. The proposed constitution of the Irish Free State had not yet been published and would not appear until the morning of polling day itself, 16 June. Few had a chance to read it before casting their votes.

184. Five days after polling-day, the results not yet in, leaders of the Republicans met at Theobald Wolfe Tone's grave at Bodenstown, County Kildare for the annual commemoration. Here Liam Mellowes, Quartermaster of the IRA and one of the Four Courts garrison, is seen addressing them.

184

190

190. Smoke from the bombardment of the besieged Four Courts drifts over Dublin, carried by a south-west wind. Before dawn on 28 June, Dublin people were awakened by the boom of 18-pounder field-guns and the crackle of rifle and machine-gun fire. They realized that the worst had happened, finding later that large parts of the city were cordoned off by the Free State Army. A short while after 1 am Free State Army men had, in a pre-emptive strike, driven two Lancia armoured cars against two of the gates of the Four Courts and left them there to block the exits. The purpose of this move was also to immobilize the Rolls-Royce 'Whippet' armoured car which the Republicans had captured in Templemore and which was now parked inside one of the Four Courts courtyards. An ultimatum calling for surrender of the position, signed by General Ennis, the Free State officer commanding the operation, was delivered to the Four Courts at 3.40 am. No reply to this was made. At 4 am the two 18-pounder field-guns that Commandant Emmett Dalton had collected from the British troops at their headquarters in Phoenix Park the previous evening, opened fire from their positions on the south bank of the Liffey at Winetavern and Bridgefoot streets. The Civil War had begun.

191. The field-gun position at the corner of Bridgefoot Street. The Free State soldiers manning the guns had time only for minimum training from Colonel Lawlor and that had been on an obsolete field-gun of a different type; they were without experience in serving 18-pounders. Not knowing how to use the sights, they simply opened the breech and sighted along the interior of the barrel. They had, however, as the photograph shows, been trained to excavate the road surface to secure a safe emplacement of the gun's 'spade', to absorb the recoil. Two Lancia armoured cars are positioned so as to give the gun-crew more cover from rifle and machine-gun fire. Evidently the danger to the hearing of the personnel involved had not been forgotten, though no ear-muffs were available for the use of the gunner who had to pull the lanyard! The guns had been handed over with only a small supply of wire-cutting high-explosive shells, such as the British army used for training purposes, which did not at first make much of an impression on the thick stone walls of the Four Courts.

191

192

192. Free State troops man a barricade commanding a lane at the back of the Four Courts. The beginning of the action was planned to be one of containment of the besieged Republican forces, in the hope that once the Four Courts garrison realized that artillery was to be used against them they would capitulate.

193. A Free State barricade near the main Republican position in O'Connell Street. Free State units were deployed in such a way that the rest of the Republican Dublin Division, occupying 'the Block' and its outposts, could be pinned down by fire, preventing them from assisting the Four Courts garrison.

193

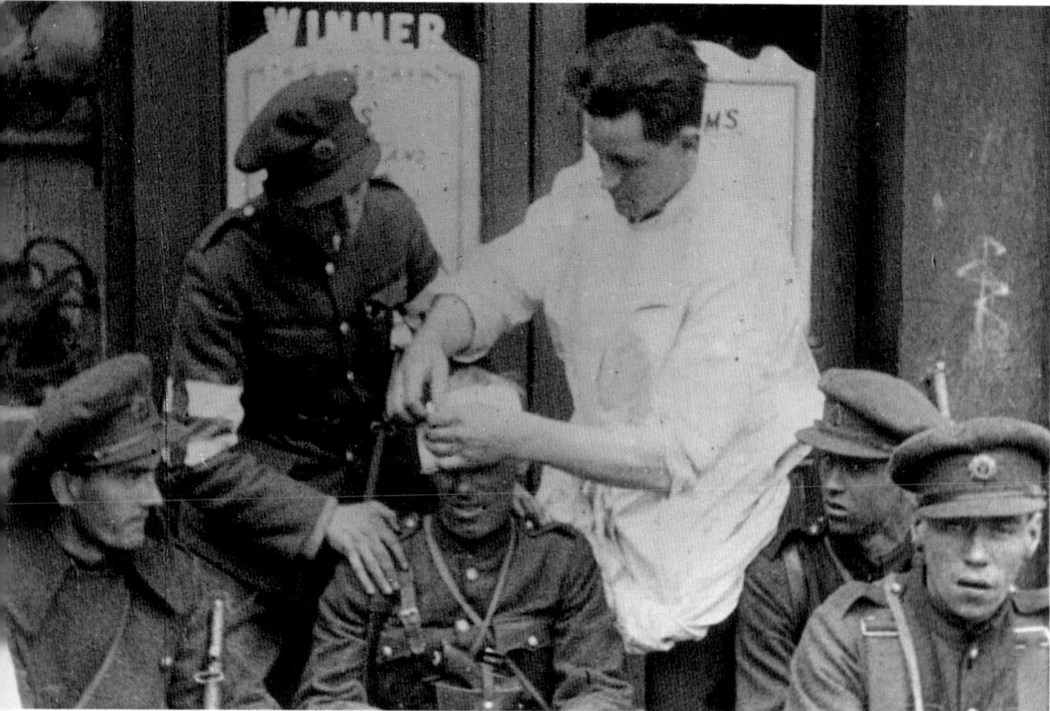

194

195

194. By June 29, the second day of the siege, casualties were mounting on both sides. Here at a Free State Army dressing station the wounded from the Four Courts operation are attended to.

195. Early in the morning of the third day of the Four Courts siege, the 18-pounder gun was brought into use to join the gun at the intersection of Winetavern Street and Merchants Quay, as part of the western end of the Four Courts had been occupied by Free State troops and the artillery fire was now being concentrated on those parts of the building still held by the Republicans. As will be seen, the rear of the building was now on fire, the flames threatening to reach the large store of munitions held in the cellars beneath the Public Records Office.

196. As the limited amount of field-gun ammunition that General Macready had at his disposal ran out, incessant demands came from the Provisional Government of the Free State for more and Macready had to send a destroyer to Carrick Fergus arsenal in Northern Ireland for further supplies. Here the shells are to be seen, just unpacked from the wood-wool in one of the packing-cases. They are still of the wire-cutting high-explosive type. Shrapnel shells had also been provided.

196

197

197. At a few minutes before 11 on the morning of 30 June, the devastating explosion of the main munitions dump took place. Although the dome of the main building was intact, fire began to spread rapidly through the Four Courts and it was clear that the garrison could not hold out for very much longer.

198. In the neighbouring deserted streets around the Four Courts, a rain of paper tatters from priceless historical documents stored in the Records Office began to fall, carried up in the explosion and miniature fire-storm from the Public Records Office, in whose cellars the explosives had been stored.

198

199

199. Around 11.30 am, through an accommodation reached with the Free State commander, General Tom Ennis, badly wounded men of the Four Courts garrison and all of the Cumann na m'Bán women were allowed to leave. Here a wounded Republican is helped to the Fire Brigade ambulance by a Free State soldier.

200. At about the same time, two Franciscan friars, Father Dominic and Father Albert were allowed to leave the building. Here, Father Dominic is seen under prisoner's escort. The priests had remained with the garrison throughout the siege in order to administer the last rites to the dying, in spite of the Irish bishop's prohibition of the last sacrament being given to Republicans under arms.

200

202

201. (Previous page) Just before 3 pm on 30 June, an order to surrender from Oscar Traynor, Commandant of the Dublin Brigade IRA was delivered to the Four Courts garrison and at 3.30 they did so. As the men lined up on the quay in front of the building for the formal surrender, a photographer prepared to take a photograph, but was prevented from doing so by Commandant Ernie O'Malley, whose intention was to spare the men humiliation, but in taking this action he unwittingly deprived them of their place in the visual history of Ireland. Later, while being kept at a temporary holding point, O'Malley escaped.

202. In this detail of the photograph on the previous page, one of the Lancia armoured cars that had been driven against the gates can be seen. The attack on the Republican positions in and around O'Connell Street was now intensified.

203. The burned-out shell of the Four Courts, 6 July 1922. Continued explosions of munitions stored in the building made it too dangerous for the fire-brigade to work and the structure was allowed to burn out. The fire reached the front of the building, the drum was gutted and the fine copper dome destroyed.

203

204. An escape plan considered by the garrison involved breaking into the sewers beneath the building, but this idea had not allowed for the fact that at high tide the sewers were flooded, as this photograph shows by the position of the high-water mark above the opening in the retaining wall. The cellars beneath the Public Record Office had been made the main repository of munitions and explosives. When the fires detonated this, the loss of Irish historical records was the worst single loss in the whole period since 1916.

205

205. Two Civic Guards look at the ruins of their station at Rathfarnham, County Dublin, on the morning of Saturday 1 July. The South Dublin Brigade of the IRA under Commandant Andrew McDonnell had received orders to retreat upon Blessington and make contact with Republicans from the south to form a body strong enough to attack the Free State GHQ in Portobello Barracks and other Free State strong-points in Dublin. They destroyed their barracks and Rathfarnham Civic Guard station on Friday night, and crossing the mountains via the Sally Gap, reached Blessington on the Saturday.

206. In order to deny the Free State Army the use of the Blessington steam tram for transport purposes, the Republicans in Blessington derailed the tram on 1 July. It was as this moment that the Civil War was strategically lost by the Republicans, for they were unable to muster a sufficiently strong and mobile force to mount a lightning attack on the Dublin headquarters and barracks of the Free State forces. The IRA South Dublin Brigade led by Michael Sheehan, with only 70 reinforcements from the south making it a completely inadequate force, began a cautious advance on Dublin that could only end in rapid failure.

206

207

207. Free State troops in a charabanc at Crooksling, South County Dublin, 5 July. The Free State Army immediately rushed forces to intercept the Republican advance at Crooksling; when the Republicans reached Crooksling, they received a dispatch from Commandant Oscar Traynor, informing them that the fighting in Dublin had ended and ordering them to go south and regroup.

208. A Free State sniper puts in another clip of ammunition while his companion takes aim towards the Hammam Hotel which formed part of 'the Block' in O'Connell Street, where Commandant Oscar Traynor and other commanding officers, including Cathal Brugha, were positioned. There had already been three attempts to secure a cease-fire: one made by the Archbishop of Dublin, one by a group of women led by Madame Maude Gonne MacBride and a third by leaders of the Labour Party. De Valera, who had joined up again as an ordinary Volunteer, had got into 'the Block' where he was concerned with all three peace moves, but all foundered on the Free State demand that the Republicans surrender their arms. A tragedy, for at the war's end, arms were not surrendered but peace came none the less.

208

209

210

209. In a laneway behind 'the Block', a Free State officer and three privates keep watch. At the beginning of the operation against 'the Block' the strategy was generally the same used in the start of the siege of the Four Courts – containment followed by bombardment. However, the first part was much more difficult as there were many more Republican outposts in hotels and other buildings scattered over quite a wide area. The maze of lanes and small houses with secret tunnels built during the Tan War at the back of 'the Block' made it possible for members of the garrison to leave and messengers to enter in spite of the Free State cordons.

210. Before the field-guns were brought into action against the Republican headquarters in O'Connell Street, sniping formed a very important part of the action. Here a Free State sniper (*on the ground*) aiming at the back of 'the Block' has a medical orderly standing around the corner in attendance.

211. During the action on 1 July, a wounded Free State soldier kept curious civilian spectators back in a safe area in the vicinity of Marlborough Street, not far from the Republican headquarters in 'the Block' on O'Connell Street.

212

213

1922

212. Moran's Hotel, Gardiner Street, Dublin, was a Republican outpost (this photograph was taken on 6 July, after the fighting was over). Before any direct assault could be made on 'the Block', the field-guns had to be brought into position, but before this could be accomplished, sniper positions in outlying Republican outposts such as this one had to be reduced.

213. A civilian ambulance of the St John's Ambulance Brigade. Unlike the more isolated position of the Four Courts, the Republican headquarters in 'the Block' was situated close to an area of tenement houses. At the start of hostilities on 28 June, the inhabitants of the tenements were trapped inside the Free State troop's cordon. The St John's Ambulance Brigade played a leading role in the evacuation of the elderly and infirm from the area of conflict.

214. An elderly man is evacuated from the danger area by St John's Ambulance Brigade men. Several schools in safe areas were turned into refuges for those who had to leave their homes.

214

215. Another obstacle to the assault on 'the Block' was the repeated necessity of bringing tenement dwellers into safety as the fighting continued. Here a parish priest leads a party of women and children to safety under a Red Cross flag.

216. An outpost in a barricaded shop, from which the Republicans withdrew early in the fighting. The defence of the Republican positions was more widely extended than in the Four Courts siege, making the deployment of heavy guns by the Free State forces more difficult.

217. An evacuated Republican outpost in a shop being occupied by Free State soldiers. Investing and occupying these positions took the Free State forces some time.

218. By 1 July, food supplies had run out in the vicinity of the fighting and a Free State Lancia armoured car was sent around distributing bread to the civilian population inside the Free State cordon.

216

217

215

218

219

219. One of the 18-pounders that had been used during the bombardment of the Four Courts, was positioned at the corner of Henry Street and O'Connell Street with its gun trained on 'the Block'. A Lancia armoured car was again being used to improve protection for the gun crew. By 2 July, when the more commanding Republican outposts had been captured and it was possible to position the guns with reasonable cover for their crews, the penultimate stage of the action commenced.

220

220. The Free State field-gun at Henry Street. As soon as the training angle had been directed to bear on 'the Block', a second armoured car was put in position to give further protection to the gun crew. The dust stirred up by the blast from the muzzle is seen in this photograph, but the crew have forgotten to protect their ears!

221

221. A window in a house opposite the Republican headquarters in O'Connell Street, shattered by a burst of machine-gun fire.

222. 'The Block' consisted of a string of hotels and shops, including the Hammam Hotel and the Gresham, mostly re-edified Georgian brick houses, which were nowhere near as strong as the solid stone structure of the Four Courts. In this photograph taken on Monday 3 July, the visible puffs of smoke are, in fact, dust from bricks pulverized by the impact of high-velocity rifle bullets, while the big gaps in the walls are the result of shelling. Once the 18-pounder shelling began there could be no doubt about the outcome. The Republican garrison in 'the Block' had been able to keep up a surprising degree of communication with the outside world through the maze of small lanes behind the buildings and through tunnels between cellars. When the bombardment began, the Republican leaders decided that their position was untenable, that most of them should evacuate and attempt to go south to link up with the intact forces of Republicans. Most of the garrison of 'the Block' as well as Oscar Traynor and de Valera succeeded in passing the Free State cordons, but Cathal Brugha elected to remain with a small force, and to continue to engage the Free State troops so that the evacuation of the other members of the garrison would not be noticed.

222

223

223. In order to convert 'the Block' into a defensive position, holes had been broken through the walls from one building to another. This had also been done to the walls of houses at the rear of 'the Block' as well as through cellars, so that the area had become a network of passageways. An interesting little detail is the empty case of Condensed Milk Company of Ireland tins of milk. This photograph was taken after the capture of the position by the Free State forces .

224. By Wednesday 5 July, the fire-field in O'Connell Street was further increased by the Vickers guns of the Rolls-Royce 'Whippets', one of which is seen here advancing towards 'the Block'. This gave additional fire-power to the Free State troops for the final stage of their attack.

224

225

225. Although O'Connell Street was now a deadly place to be, neither side fired upon the St John's Ambulance men, here seen attending a casualty.

226. The bombardment on Wednesday 5 July, had quickly made breaches in the brick walls of 'the Block', and the next phase of the assault began. Protected by the increased covering fire, Free State soldiers from a Lancia, led by an officer, have entered a breach and are planting an incendiary device in the wreckage within the building.

226

227

227. At the other end of 'the Block', on the same day, a Free State soldier prepares a petrol bomb to fling into a lower window of the Gresham Hotel.

228. Very soon fire spread rapidly through the block and the Hammam Hotel was ablaze; the rear-guard garrison, under Cathal Brugha, was still holding out.

229. The Gresham Hotel was soon burning like a furnace. Cathal Brugha ordered the remaining members of the garrison, both men and women, to surrender but he remained inside with Dr Brennan, the medical officer of the garrison and Nurse Linda Kearns. A little later, he emerged with two pistols at the ready, advancing on the Free State soldiers in the lane. Everyone on both sides called on him to surrender but he opened fire and a moment later fell riddled with bullets. Nurse Kearns held a severed artery in his arm as he was rushed to hospital. By the evening, the fighting in Dublin was over.

228

229

230

230. Two Free State 'Whippets' patrol smoke-filled O'Connell Street, Dublin on the evening of 5 July. There remained only the taking into custody of Republican soldiers who were in outlying positions but who had been ordered to surrender.

231. A Free State Army marksman, from the shelter afforded by the front of a Lancia in Parnell Street, gives cover to a search party rounding up any remaining Republican Army men on 5 July.

232. A rifleman of a Free State platoon searching for Republicans, breaks open the door of a house in Moore Lane, off Parnell Street on the same evening.

233. The prisoners were loaded into Lancia armoured cars and lorries on 5 July to be brought to barracks and prisons. In this photograph a wounded prisoner is handing down a note to a Free State officer while a Republican Cumann na m'Bán woman looks on.

231

232

233

234

234. Covered by a party of Free State soldiers, the last Republican soldiers leave an outpost in O'Connell Street on 5 July.

235. Cathal Brugha lies in state, Saturday 8 July 1922. Although given the best care available at the time, he died on 7 July. His loss was to be the most sincerely mourned on both sides. From 1916 onwards he had gained a reputation for courage, single-mindedness and incorruptibility and he remains one of the most loved and revered figures in the struggle for Irish freedom. A very poignant note is struck by the fact that, for this small man, in the exigencies of the situation no Volunteer Officer's uniform of sufficiently small size could be found. Two members of Cumann na m'Bán in full uniform compose his Guard of Honour.

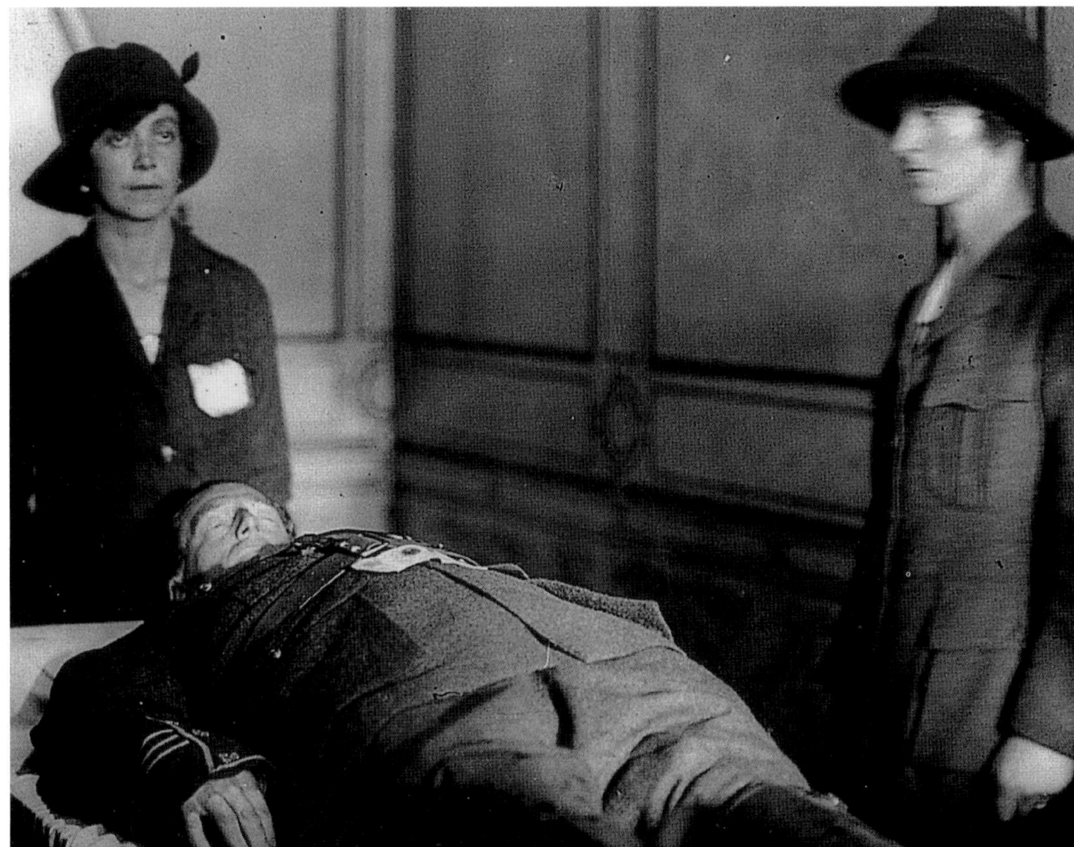

235

236

237

236. A Free State officer searches a suspected Republican in a Dublin back street. Once again, sudden arrests and searches were commonplace in the streets of Dublin. Once again the knock on the door by night was dreaded. Once more the cells of Mountjoy and Kilmainham prisons were full again and internment camps were opening.

237. At the funeral of Cathal Brugha, more women than men were in attendance. On the extreme right is seen the tragic face of Mary MacSwiney, in front of her, bare-headed, Muriel MacSwiney, and between the two figures on the left of the photograph is a very interesting detail in the background; Cumann na m'Bán women with linked hands, undertaking the work of crowd control in place of Republican police or of the Free State Civic Guards.

238

238. A Republican prisoner being marched to Mountjoy Goal under the escort of Free State soldiers, July 1922. The fighting in Dublin had stopped but everyone knew, in spite of the military censorship of the press, that it was still going on out of the hearing and sight of Dubliners.

239. Michael Collins in Free State Army uniform, Portobello Barracks, Dublin, 15 July 1922. At this moment a very significant event occurred. The Provisional Government under the chairmanship of Michael Collins had prorogued a meeting of the Dail but on 15 July the Provisional Government formed a war council and Michael Collins, who already held the position corresponding to Taoseach, became Commander-in-Chief of the military forces of the Free State. This is the earliest photograph of Michael Collins in Free State Army uniform. He had now reached the apogee of his power.

239

By the time the fighting in Dublin was over, the Civil War was lost and won, but was far from being ended. Deprived almost completely of the information derived from Michael Collins's superb intelligence machine, the loose-knit Republican command had neither the ability to make wide-ranging strategic decisions nor an adequate intelligence-gathering capability of its own. Faced with the well-supplied Free State Army with its artillery, armoured cars, weapons and munitions, as well as training by the British, the Republicans' only chance would have been a mass attack on Dublin carried out at the very start of the fighting, but they lacked the united command structure, the transport and the weaponry. The arms seizures, such as that from the SS *Upnor*, were only of rifles, machine-guns and mines. Such acquisitions served merely to prolong the war without determining its outcome, as did the extended line fighting which the Free State began at once to roll up from its flanks. Most important of all, the solid support of the mass of the Irish people had been eroded, so that a really long guerrilla war was out of the question. The tremendous bravery and tenacity of the leaders of the Republicans in the face of what was a hopeless situation is a most tragic aspect of this phase of the war.

240. Somewhere in County Limerick, sometime in July – this carefully composed propaganda photograph was taken as material for Desmond FitzGerald's effectively conducted media campaign on behalf of the Free State Provisional Government.

Fighting in the Country

Hostilities continue

241

1922

241. Republican forces in Carrick-on-Suir preparing barricades on 20 July 1922 to defend the town against the advancing Free State Army. At this time, the Irish Republican Army held an area of the south of Ireland whose northern border ran, roughly, from Enniscorthy to Kilkenny and across to Limerick, with pockets of Republican resistance in counties Galway, Mayo, Sligo, Leitrim and Donegal. It was not long before the Free State Army, well armed now with rifles, machine-guns, armoured cars and field-guns and with a considerable number of heavy lorries, were on the offensive. Apart from the superiority in *matériel* that the Free State Army had acquired, the IRA had been trained as a guerrilla force and it should have been understood by the Republican command staff that their strength lay in this form of fighting, not in holding battle lines across the island. It is, of course, so easy to be complacently wise after the event, but none the less, a failure to foresee the outcome of such a profound change of strategy must surely be considered as one of the fundamental errors of judgement on the Republican side.

242. An IRA sentry on duty at the doorway of the Bank of Ireland, Carrick-on-Suir, 20 July 1922.

243. General Prout, the commanding officer of the Free State forces who turned the Republican lines in Wexford and Waterford on his arrival in Carrick-on-Suir early in August. The Republican forces changed their minds about defending the town and Carrick-on-Suir was fortunate in escaping with very little damage. Prout established his headquarters in the town and from here, prepared to advance further. The pressure of the well-led, well-trained and well-equipped Free State Army could not be withstood on either the eastern or the western end of the Republican forces' extended front lines.

242

243

244

244. A Free State armoured car (*on the right*) and partly uniformed soldiers in Claregalway on 20 July. In the west, the Free State forces under General Sean MacKeon were preparing to encounter the more appropriate guerrilla-style of fighting that had been begun by the IRA in that area. Here the Free State forces found themselves undergoing experiences that had been the lot of the Crown Forces a little over a year before. The Republicans in Connaught had been very active on 30 June and had taken Ennis and Castlebar. They also destroyed the Marconi transmitter at Clifden, a foolish act, since it could have been useful.

245. A company of Free State troops near the bridge at Killaloe in late July. The main area of operations was against the Republican enclave of the south-west which became known, briefly, as the 'Munster Republic'. Michael Collins was now Commander-in-Chief of the Free State Army and immediately under him was General O'Duffy, the General Officer Commanding, South-western Command. During the fighting for Limerick city, O'Duffy made his headquarters at the Lake Hotel, Killaloe, seen in the background, where there was an important bridge over the wide and deep Shannon river.

245

246

247

248

249

246. General William Murphy, who had served as an officer in the British Army, was appointed by O'Duffy to lead the Free State advance from Limerick towards counties Cork and Kerry.

247. The Republicans withdrew from their last positions in Limerick, having set fire to the barracks on Friday 21 July. The city was taken over by the Free State forces on the following day and suffered very little damage. Here are Free State soldiers and transport vehicles as well as a Rolls-Royce 'Whippet' named 'Danny Boy'. All the armoured cars were given names. It will be seen that the protective doors in front of its radiator are closed and the Vickers machine-gun is pointed straight at the photographer!

248. Very little comfort was available at first in the wrecked barracks, some of which were mere burnt-out shells. Here a troop of young Free State soldiers keep warm around a fire lit in an old tin-bath. From the careless way in which their rifles are disposed one can see how little training they have had, and the ammunition slings, made of canvas and cord tell their own tale too.

249. A Free State barricade erected on the road leading out of Limerick to Adare, 23 July. Barricades were erected on the roads leading out of the city to the south as a primary defence against a counter-attack taking place while the Free State forces were regrouping before recommencing their advance. This photograph, like others that we will encounter later, has the air of a set-piece. Desmond FitzGerald (father of a Taoseach-to-be), who had so ably organized publicity for Sinn Fein in 1919, 1920 and 1921, was in charge of the Free State media propaganda. He had a genius way ahead of his time for this sort of work and it is largely thanks to his efforts that we have so many photographs of the Free State side of the campaign, although, occasionally, some may appear a little contrived.

251

250. Free State troops in occupation of King John's Castle, Limerick, in late July 1922. As it was one of the strongest buildings in Limerick, commanding an important bridge over the Shannon and riverside roads, a Free State garrison was left in there until all risk of a Republican counter-offensive was over.

251. By the beginning of July it was plain that the IRA was going to offer stiffer resistance to the Free State forces to the south of Limerick. Here a Free State Army Medical Corps prepares its equipment for use in the advance upon Kilmallock. The man in a cap at the extreme right of the photograph shows the improvised ammunition bandoliers that were in very common use, even on the better equipped Free State side.

252

252. A Free State Army Medical Corps Model T passes through Kilmallock under a Red Cross flag just after the town had been taken by the Free State Army for the first time on Monday 31 July.

253. A Free State Army medical orderly treats a minor hand injury during the advance to Kilmallock. Model T Fords were extensively used as ambulances and for carrying medical supplies. Note the oil lamp used as a rear light.

253

254

254. Sunday 30 July – a bridge across a small tributary of the River Maigue, blown up by Republicans retreating on Bruree, has just been filled in by Free State Army troops so that one of General Murphy's 18-pounder field-guns can be towed across, hitched to the tail of a lorry commandeered in Limerick.

255

255. This photograph, allegedly of the fighting in the vicinity of Bruree, entirely fails to convince. Just see what superb targets most of the group make and with what care their leather leggings have been polished, in the heat of action too!

256. Another example of a posed propaganda photograph taken of Free State troops. Posed photographs such as this appear to be a propaganda feature of all military campaigns. Its original caption was 'Somewhere in the South West'.

256

257. How different is this photograph of a Free State soldier who has just suffered a hit in the head during the Bruree fighting on 30 July.

258. Compare, too, this shot taken on the same day, of another soldier with a head wound being tended by Free State Army medical orderlies wearing improvised Red Cross armbands. Note the low view-point, resulting from the photographer lying prone on the road. Observe also that the light is overcast and dull, in contrast to the ideal photographic conditions seen in the propaganda photograph 255.

257

258

259

1922

259. Free State Army troops advancing from Bruree towards Newcastle West on 6 August 1922, in pursuit of the retreating Republican forces now threatened in their rear by Free State troops which had landed in Kerry and Cork.

260. A service for the dead held in the morgue at Portobello Barracks, Dublin, on Friday 6 August for Free State soldiers killed in the fighting south of Limerick.

261. Women leaving the morgue after the service.

260

261

262

262. The most active opposition of the Republican forces was now taking place in Galway, Mayo, Sligo and Leitrim. In this posed Republican propaganda photograph is a company of the Second Western Division IRA in Leitrim. On 12 July they captured a Rolls-Royce 'Whippet' named 'Ballinalee' at Drumkeen, so-called because this was the area in which General Sean MacKeon, known as the 'Blackmith of Ballinalee' was in charge of the Free State Army operations. Of all the commanders in the Civil War he had shown the greatest humanity in the treatment of prisoners, a reputation he had first gained in the Tan War.

263. Campbell's Field, Swinford, County Mayo – taken on 2 August of Free State soldiers as prisoners. They had been captured a few days earlier in the old Constabulary Barracks when the town of Swinford fell to the IRA.

263

264

264. Free State prisoners playing hurley in Campbell's Field, guarded by an armed IRA man.

265. One of the captured Free State soldiers whose wounded hands had been dressed by Tom Murray, Chief Medical Officer, East Mayo Brigade of the IRA.

265

266

266. The Free State Army troops landing at Fenit, County Kerry on 2 August. The landing actually took place at 2 am and this would seem to be a reconstruction of the event organized on behalf of Desmond FitzGerald. The troops had left Dublin early on the first of the month on board the B & I passenger vessel SS *Lady Wicklow* chartered for the purpose.

The resources at the disposal of the Provisional Government far exceeded those of the Republicans, making it possible for the Free State Army to turn the Republican flank and to land forces behind their lines in a way that rendered formal battle-lines an essentially impractical tactical manoeuvre. An even bigger sea-borne force was on the way.

267

267. General Tom Ennis and General Mulcahy at the Free State Army headquarters, Portobello Barracks, 7 August, just before they set out for the North Wall. A much more extensive sea-borne landing had been planned, which General Ennis was to command in the field and which General Emmett Dalton was to coordinate overall. Two vessels were to be used this time: the *Lady Wicklow* and the London & North Western Railway Company's steamer SS *Arvonia* ex *Cambria*. These were standing by at the North Wall, Dublin, in the vicinity of the great Titan crane.

268. The *Arvonia* at her berth at the North Wall, Dublin. A leg of the giant Titan crane can be seen in the middle of the photograph. Aboard the *Arvonia*, as well as armoured cars and an 18-pounder field-gun, were 450 Free State Army men and officers, most of whom were to be ordered below decks as the approach to the landing area at Passage West, Cork, was in progress.

269

269. Free State troops boarding the SS *Arvonia*, while a Lancia armoured car is lifted on board by the giant crane, which had earlier made light work of loading one of the very much heavier twin-turret 'Peerless' armoured cars on to its deck. Note, on the left, the wall of sandbags piled along the ship's rail in anticipation of a contested landing at Cork.

270. To arrive at their destination at the right time, the *Arvonia* and the *Lady Wicklow* left their berths by the Titan crane (*top right of the photograph*), a little after noon on 7 August.

271. (Overleaf) With a deck cargo of armoured cars, an 18-pounder field-gun and 450 troops aboard, conditions on the *Arvonia* were crowded. It has been said that a number of the newly enlisted Free State soldiers had never handled a weapon before and had to be given elementary instructions during the voyage; this photograph tends to bear this out. Under Colonel Lawlor's training, the gunners were clearly more experienced and are engaged in cleaning their field-piece. The *Arvonia*, ex *Cambria*, propelled by a powerful triple-expansion marine compound engine, could make a top speed of 21 knots.

270

FOUR
COURTS

272. Watched by the captain and the first officer of the *Arvonia*, General Dalton and General Ennis confer on deck during the afternoon of 7 August. General Mulcahy had placed the command of this operation in the hands of General Emmett Dalton and immediately under him, General Tom Ennis. The vessels had been commandeered on a charter basis and the Captain of the *Arvonia*, most unhappy at the use of his vessel as a troopship, was quite convinced that he was on the *Arvonia's* last voyage. He did not consider the plan, worked out by Collins, Mulcahy and Dalton, to be a feasible one, and was convinced that they would be sunk by mines as soon as they entered Cork Harbour. During that night the vessels were shadowed by British warships and challenged by them, but Dalton sent back signals begging the British not to disclose their presence or whereabouts.

273. A very young recruit on the *Arvonia* writes a letter home during the voyage. The huge numbers of unemployed now found in Ireland had promoted enlistment in the Free State Army and as all reserves were being pressed into service, there were not enough uniforms to go round, as can be seen from the young man in civilian clothes with a rifle and a canvas bandolier at the left of the photograph.

272

273

275

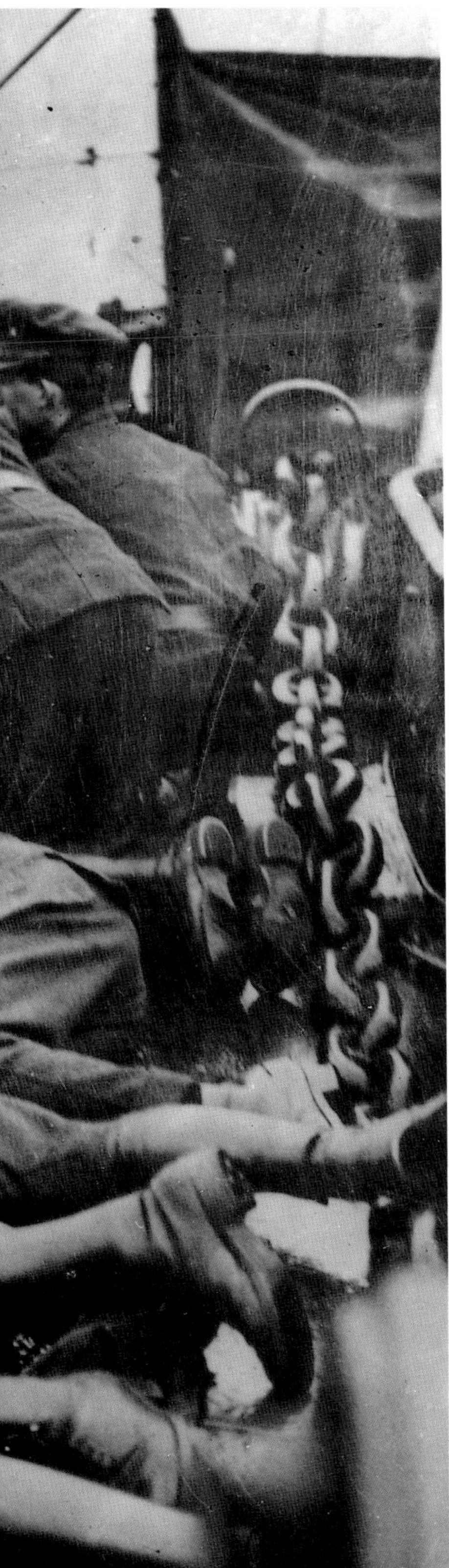

274

274. On board the *Arvonia* a machine-gunner on an armoured car puts in some practice, but, curiously enough, without an ammunition pan in place on his Lewis gun. He is watched by the ship's disapproving first officer. This and the next three photographs would seem to have been set pieces prepared for Desmond FitzGerald's well-oiled propaganda machine.

275. Here the machine-gunners have put their Lewis gun ammunition-pans in place and have one in reserve, but what can be the purpose of pointing side-arms at an empty horizon; all very dramatic but hardly convincing.

277

276. This posturing on the top of a 'Peerless' is singularly unconvincing.

277. While it is possible that this adaptive use of a field-gun might have been seriously considered, one has to ask what means had been used to secure the spade to the steel deck in the event of the gun being fired. Neglect of this could have resulted in injury to those nearby. On the whole this looks like more propaganda.

278

1922

278. This scene on the bridge cannot have been taken at the time when the vessel was close to its destination. The *Arvonia* and the *Lady Wicklow* arrived in Cork Harbour at around 2 am on 8 August, in darkness. General Dalton then sent a reconnaissance party ashore in a motor boat under Frank O'Friel, to discover if the proposed point of disembarkation at Passage West was secure. There are a number of singular aspects of this part of the operation. General Dalton had taken on a local pilot who Dalton alleges had Republican sympathies and had to be threatened with a pistol before he would bring them to a safe, mine-free, berth. But with block-ships sunk in the fairway, how had such an essential wharf, furnished with a crane, as that at the Cork Shipbuilding Company's premises at Passage West neither have been mined nor defended by an adequate force of Republicans, and how did the pilot know that this was the case? It looks very much as though the whole situation in Cork Harbour had been organized in advance through the connivance of some collaborators in the local IRA; this possibility should not be disregarded when personalities such as Collins and Dalton were in play.

279. We are certainly back to actuality material here, with the *Arvonia* manœuvering cautiously past the block-ships to get to Passage West, but notice that the block-ships seem to have been sunk in shallow water at the East side of the fairway. It all looks rather odd.

280

280. Free State troops leaving the *Arvonia* at Passage West on the morning of 8 August. But who are the two civilians being allowed to watch a secret military operation at such close quarters?

281

281. As soon as a small shore party was landed, the next task was to land an armoured car and the field-guns. The field-guns had to be unloaded first because the heavy 'Peerless' car could not be brought ashore until the tide had fallen sufficiently to make the deck of the *Arvonia* flush with the level of the wharf.

283

282. The *Arvonia's* winches and derricks could handle the field-guns, but for the heavy armoured cars there was no Titan crane as there had been in Dublin and the only crane available was not strong enough to lift and swing the heavy cars ashore.

283. When the tide had made the *Arvonia's* deck level with the wharf, heavy baulks of timber were laid from ship to shore and with the crane supporting the front of the 'Peerless', it was driven until the front wheels were ashore.

284

284. This photograph shows the completion of the task of getting the heavy 'Peerless' ashore. When the front wheels were on the wharf, the slings of the crane were transferred to the rear of the vehicle, the crane took up as much weight as possible and the car was driven across the wooden baulks on to the wharf.

285. A Lancia, packed with Free State soldiers, tows an 18-pounder gun from the wharf. The advance on Cork city could now begin. It was this operation and that at Fenit which relieved the pressure on the Free State forces around Kilmallock and Bruree in County Limerick.

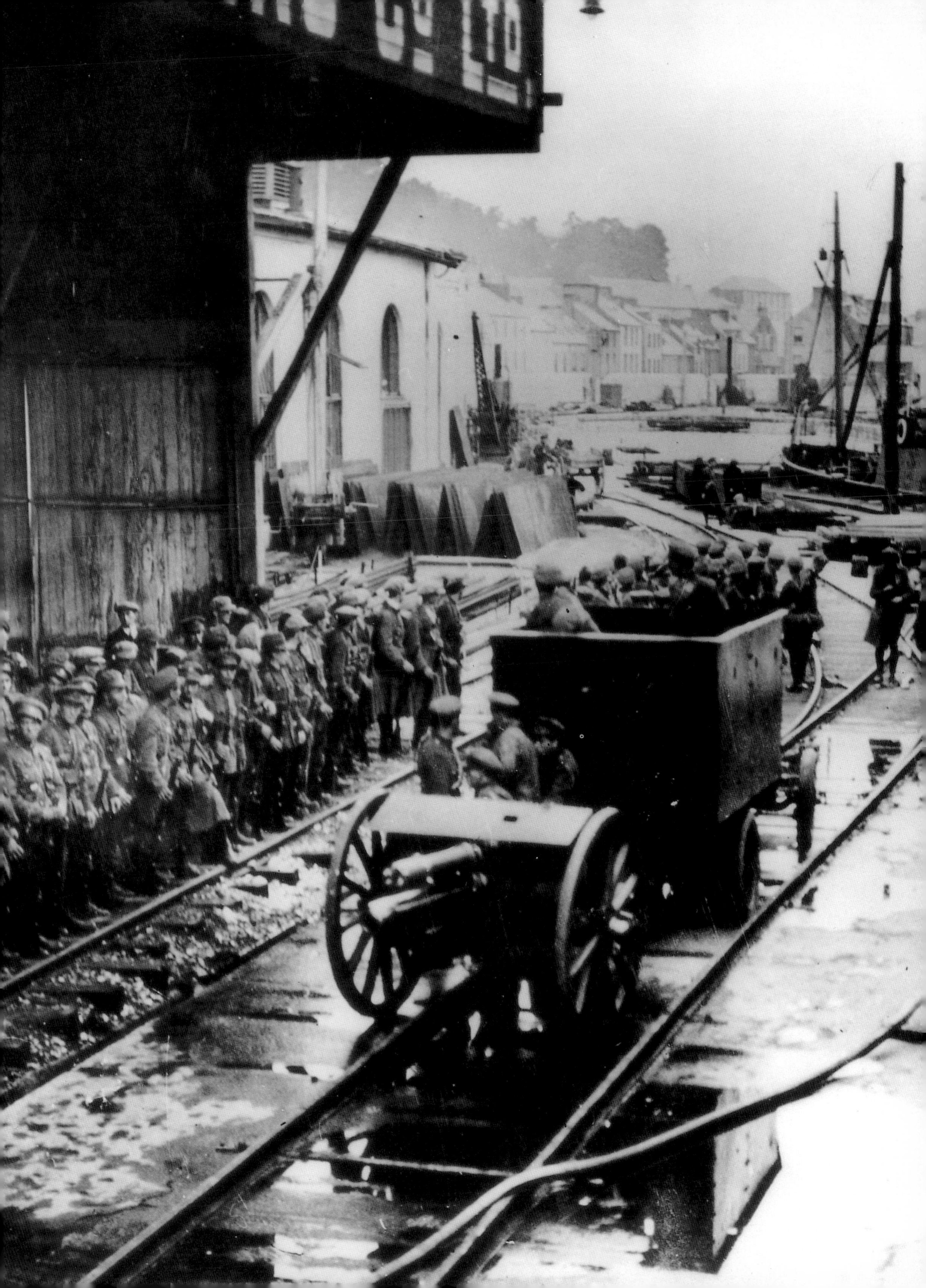

286

1922

286. The funeral cortege of Arthur Griffith passing down O'Connell Street in Dublin. His sudden death as a result of a stroke on the morning of 12 August brought sincere sorrow to both Free State and Republican supporters, in spite of the bitterness of the Civil War. This event was one of the psychological moments when an effort to end the Civil War might have been attempted with more chance of success than would have been possible at any later time. The effort was not made.

287

287. Michael Collins (*facing towards camera at left*), Chairman of the Provisional Government and Commander-in-Chief of the Free State Army at the funeral of Arthur Griffith. Although it has been written of Collins that he did not show sorrow at the funeral, both the still and motion-picture records demonstrate this observation to be completely inaccurate.

288

1922

288. On the last day of his life, 22 August 1922, Michael Collins gets into his Leyland open tourer staff-car at Skibbereen, County Cork, to commence his journey back to Cork. He was to pass within less than five miles of de Valera, who had come expressly to West Cork to attempt a meeting with him. There was a feeling that a peace move might be initiated and de Valera himself was convinced that the war should be ended as soon as possible; but that meeting was not to take place. Within a couple of hours Collins would be dead, under circumstances that have, to this day, never found an entirely satisfactory explanation. The officer commanding the convoy, General Emmett Dalton, brought his body back to Cork, arriving just after midnight.

289

289. Collins's body lies in a hurriedly prepared private room in Shanakiel Hospital, Cork, the back of his head blown away by a large calibre bullet.

290

290. In great-coat and cap (*on the right*), Commandant Frank O'Friel (he had been promoted to that rank in the field by General Emmett Dalton), and (*in front of him*) General Tom Ennis watch as the body of Michael Collins, in a temporary coffin, is embarked aboard the commandeered TSS *Classic* at Penrose Quay, Cork, on the afternoon of 23 August. The vessel, normally running between Cork and Fishguard Harbour, had been chartered to perform this service as the most secure way of returning the body to Dublin.

291. (Overleaf) Michael Collins's body in its second coffin, on a gun-carriage outside the Pro-Cathedral, Marlborough Street, Dublin, after the celebration of a Requiem Mass on 28 August. Well over 2,000 feet of motion-picture film was shot covering this event, making it the most extensively covered funeral ever to take place in Ireland until recent times.

1922

292

292. In this little cottage in the hills near Ballyvourney in West Cork, the Republican Director of Propaganda, Erskine Childers, continued to bring out the newspaper *An Pûblacht.* But the propaganda battle had largely been won by his opposite number on the Free State side, Desmond FitzGerald, whose feeling for the importance of photographs had grown all the time. It is strange that Childers, whose wife had given us the incomparable photographic coverage of the voyage of the *Asgard* (*see pages 85–6*) should have lost his sense of the importance of the photographic actuality in communications and propaganda, leaving us with pitifully few photographic records on the Republican side of the struggle.The 'Munster Republic' had now shrunk to pockets of resistance in remote areas and it was clear to the Republican command that the war could only be continued as a guerrilla operation.

293. Kevin O'Higgins, Minister for Home Affairs, the youngest member of the Executive Council was only 30. During his rapid rise in importance he had been closest to Cosgrave and to Blythe. In the ensuing months he was to support more strongly even than General Mulcahy the introduction and operation of the draconian Special Powers, vigorously resisted by Thomas Johnson and the Labour Party, who were now the only opposition in the Provisional Parliament. These Special Powers were to lead to 77 executions, that would leave the people of Ireland more embittered than even the exigencies of Civil War had, up to now, occasioned. The first four executions took place on 17 November 1922. A strict censorship of the press had also been introduced and this was followed a few months later by film censorship. War and censorship go hand in hand.

293

294

294. The Executive Council of the Provisional Government in session, Government Buildings, Dublin, October 1922. After the death of Collins, the Provisional Government was headed by William T. Cosgrave as President of the Executive Council and General Mulcahy became Commander-in-Chief as well as Minister for Defence. A hardening of attitudes to the Republicans followed. Collins had helped to restrain this tendency, but a more severe attitude was now to come about mostly through the influence of General Mulcahy and of Kevin O'Higgins, seen here second from the right. On his right sits Ernest Blythe, Minister for Local Government. After a debate in the Provisional Parliament, an amnesty was issued which would last until 15 October for all who would give up their arms and undertake not to renew the fight against the Provisional Government. At the same time, however, a measure was instituted setting up military courts, with regulations which made the death penalty mandatory for the possession of arms and a number of other offences. This latter measure was strongly opposed by the Irish Labour Party. The new Special Powers were also to come into operation on 15 October, at the end of the amnesty period.

295. Erskine Childers. On 25 October, a meeting of the Republican Council of State was held in Dublin at which a Provisional Republican government, led by Eamon de Valera, was formed; Erskine Childers was summoned from West Cork to act as secretary to that body. Making his way with great difficulty through the Free State lines, he elected to spend a night (10 November) at his cousin Robert Barton's house at Annamoe in County Wicklow, before entering Dublin. At two in the morning the house was raided by Free State troops and Childers arrested in possession of a small Colt automatic pistol which had been given him by Michael Collins. Tried by military court, in camera, under the new Special Powers, he was condemned to death on 17 November. Although his case was still under appeal he was executed by shooting at Beggars Bush Barracks just after dawn (at his request) on 24 November. Thus died one of the cleverest and most able Republican figures, whose living presence would have had far-reaching consequences on the modern history of Ireland. Jurists in Ireland and in England, regard this particular execution as a judicial murder, for the victim was executed before his legitimate appeal, which had been granted, could be heard.

296. Brigadier Sean Hayles, photographed an instant before he was shot on 7 December. A representative of the Free State parliament elected in June 1922 which was not summoned to meet until 9 September, Hayles had voted for the granting of Special Powers to the Free State Army. The judicial murder of Erskine Childers, son of an English father and an Irish mother, whose wholehearted devotion to Irish independence was so widely known, made the IRA Executive decide upon a policy of summary shooting of prominent Free State figures. Because of the manner of Childers's death, the conflict in Ireland entered an increasingly grim and deadly phase. Before hostilities ended there were to be 77 executions of Republican prisoners held by the Free State.

296

295

297

298

297. Rory O'Connor. On the night of 7 December, Rory O'Connor, Liam Mellowes, Joseph Mckelvey and Richard Barrett, prisoners in Mountjoy Gaol, Dublin, were awakened and told that they would be shot at dawn the following morning, as it was officially expressed; 'As a reprisal for the assassination of Brigadier Sean Hayles TD, as a solemn warning to those associated with them who are engaged in the conspiracy of assassination against the Representatives of the Irish People' [sic].

298. From the time that he had been a member of Fianna na h'Éireann, Liam Mellowes had devoted his life to the cause of Socialism and Irish National Independence. He had been a member of the Irish Volunteers since their formation, serving in the west of Ireland during the 1916 Rising, been a Dail member in the First and Second Dails, had supported the Republican side at the time of the Treaty division, been appointed Director of Purchases for the IRA and been a leading member of the Four Courts garrison. His strong affiliation with Labour and left-wing politics made his execution a serious blow to the evolution of the left in Ireland and this fact may have influenced the decisions of those determined upon his execution.

299. Joseph McKelvey was Deputy Chief of Staff of the IRA. At the army Convention meeting of 18 July, he was among those who parted company with Liam Lynch and departed, with Rory O'Connor, to the Four Courts, where he was appointed Chief of Staff.

300. Richard Barrett, the fourth man to be executed. These executions, coming so soon after that of Erskine Childers, made it certain that a campaign of authoritarian terror had begun. This attempt to terrorize the IRA leadership was a piece of psychological ineptitude on the part of the Free State Executive Council in general and, more specifically, on the part of General Mulcahy and Kevin O'Higgins. It was extended over a period of seven months, taking, in all, 77 lives, but completely failed in its intended effect. The measure greatly increased the bitterness of the campaign and probably extended the duration of the fighting. It seems a great pity that General Sean McKeon had no seat on the Executive Council of the Free State government, for his strong influence might easily have resulted in a more humane as well as a more effective policy.

299

300

When the fighting ceases in a civil war, peace does not return. Distrust and hatred permeate a riven country. The violent imposition of a regime or an ideology always produces a mass-psychological rebound, which is certain to reactivate tensions and endanger stability for years to come. Although, in Ireland, we were misguided enough to fall into the pit of civil war, we were, in one way, saved from the worst by the fact that there was substantial intervention only on one side, by the supplying of *matérial de guerre*; think how we would have suffered if this had taken place on both sides! This is perhaps the chief reason why the Irish Civil War entailed the loss of only some 700 lives; even one is too many but imagine what could have occurred if support from outside had been equally divided. We have been luckier than most countries that have fallen into civil war in the twentieth century. This final section shows our gradual recovery from the savage hatreds of 1923.

301. Two secretaries at work in the Republican Party headquarters, Suffolk Street, Dublin in December 1922. While the military fight was in continuous decline, Republican women took up the fight in the field of public relations with extraordinary energy and determination. Many were heroines of the struggle against the British during the Tan War, which caused the Executive Council and O'Higgins, as Minister For Home Affairs , to be uncomfortable with the idea of imprisoning them. This hesitancy soon passed and the staff had to be replaced as arrests were made. As the prisons and the camps filled with Republican prisoners, an untiring effort was made by the women to keep the prisoners' fate and the conditions under which they were kept continuously before the public as is shown by the posters on the wall behind the secretaries.

End and Aftermath

The painful recovery

DO YOU
WISH HIM TO BE DETAINED
UNTIL THERE IS
NO HOPE OF HIS RECOVERY ?
IRELAND WILL WEEP FOR BRIAN NA BANBAN
SPEAK IN TIME AND
SAVE HIM.
"LE PETIT JOURNAL," an important French Paper, has this picture as its front page on October 28th. Written underneath is—
"Following the example of the Lord Mayor of Cork, four hundred and twenty-four Irishmen in Mountjoy Prison, Dublin, being refused their liberty, have decided to Hunger Strike. In vain their gaolers try to make them yield by offering them abundant food. Since the 14th october the prisoners resolutely maintain their terrible decision."
DO YOU REALISE YOUR
RESPONSIBILITY ?
Denis Barry
OTHER TRAGEDIES
IMMINENT
DYING
TINTOWN 2 CAMP
SIGN THE
PLEBISCITE
DO NOT DELAY

302

1923

302. A street demonstration by Republican women in Dorset Street, Dublin in December 1922. Because strict censorship of the press was in operation, Republican women had to use every means in their power to get their message about the fate and conditions of Republican prisoners across; they did this in spite of the harassment and imprisonment that became their lot. Street demonstrations of this kind had been illegal in Padraic Pearse's time and were now illegal once again.

303. Another Republican women's demonstration in Dublin, this time in early April 1923. The transition of the fighting into an anti-guerrilla war led to increasing summary executions of prisoners in the field and the only way in which the public could be made aware of this was by public marches and demonstrations such as this; it was also the only way that the new underground civil administration, headed by de Valera, could effectively communicate. This public action by the Cumman na m'Bán was the means whereby ordinary people became aware of the widespread deterioration of the struggle and of the number of prominent individuals who had died under mysterious circumstances, including Sean Lemass, the brother of a future prime minister, seized by Free State Special Branch men in July. His body was found on the Featherbed Mountain with marks of torture in October. It is now thought that this killing was committed by much feared Special Branch detectives in Oriel House.

304. (Overleaf) Can it be odd that children, surrounded by an atmosphere of violence and terror, should adapt their games to act out their fears and aspirations. But the spurs and the rifle have gone and in their place has come the machine-gun.

RETREAT
SACRED HEART SODALITY
KEYSTONE AND GILPIN
Dispatch
IN HONOUR OF THE MURDERED REPUBLICANS WHOSE MURDERERS HAVE NOT BEEN BROUGHT TO JUSTICE
RORY O'CONNOR
LIAM MELLOWES
JOE McKELVEY
DICK BARRETT
HEROES AND MARTYRS
NOEL LEMASS ... MURDERED ... ON THE DUBLIN MOUNTS.
HARRY BOLAND MURDERED IN BALBRIGGAN
AT CABRA

305

1923

305. Timothy Healy, the first Governor General of the Irish Free State. On 6 December, a year exactly after the signing of the Articles of Agreement for a Treaty, the Irish Free State came officially into being, and its Governor General Timothy Healy, was appointed by King George V at the nomination of the Provisional Government. Healey had had an outstanding career at the Bar and had been the most important member of the Irish Parliamentary Party to oppose Parnell.

306. General Tom Ennis and President Cosgrave at Dublin Castle in early 1923. There was now, in effect, something closely approaching a military dictatorship, with General Mulcahy as both Commander-in-Chief and Minister for Defence. Under the Special Powers, all the amenities and safeguards of civilian life had been suspended indefinitely, including *habeas corpus* and the Coroners' Courts. The government of the Free State was now very much in the hands of the military.

307

1923

307. The ruins of Palmerston House, seat of the Earl of Mayo, Straffan, County Kildare. As 1923 began, the character of the fighting changed as the Republican forces were pushed further and further into isolated pockets of resistance. Attacks continued by the Republican Army Executive on the property of those who were considered to be influential supporters of the of the Free State. Lord Mayo's house in County Kildare was one of those destroyed by fire on 29 January 1923; a sad event when one considers that it was in this house that the great blind Irish bard O'Carolan was so many times entertained by John, the fourth Earl and, in gratitude, left us one of his loveliest compositions, *Lord Mayo.*

308. The houses of prominent members of the Free State Government also came under attack. Here is the house of the Chief State Solicitor, Mr Corrigan, who is himself seen amid the wreckage left by the explosion of a Republican bomb on 29 January. These attacks were made in retaliation for the summary executions which were still continuing.

309

1923

309. Nor were these attacks confined to the country or suburbs. Sean McGarry, a member of the IRB from before the Easter Rising and representative of a Dublin constituency in the Free State Dail, was targeted because he had voted for the Special Powers. His shop (*seen here*) was destroyed by a bomb in February 1923. Earlier, on 10 December 1922, his house had been set ablaze before it had been completely evacuated, resulting in the severe injury and subsequent death of his young son from burns.

310

310. The ruins of Kilmessan station on the Midland Great Western Railway, destroyed by Republicans on Tuesday, 23 January 1923. Although Carrick-on-Suir was briefly retaken by the Republicans and lost again, the only major strategic capability left to them was that of attacks on the railways. Most of the country's main railway bridges had already been destroyed, but stations, minor bridges and trains were attacked.

312

311. Engineers and railway officials examine a partly destroyed bridge on the Midland Great Western Dublin to Galway line, near Dublin in mid-March 1923.

312. The wreck of the down Midland Great Western Galway Express near Edenderry Junction, derailed by the IRA on 17 February 1923. It was by now very evident to de Valera and the underground Republican government that he had formed around him, that the Republican military campaign had no future, but the Republican civil administration had no power over the IRA Executive which was determined to carry on.

313. (Overleaf) An Athlone housewife gets water from a watercart. On 23 February 1923, the IRA destroyed the waterworks at Athlone, leaving the town with only emergency supplies. The increasingly negative and destructive character of the IRA operations was beginning to effect morale on the Republican side, as it expressed a sense of hopelessness among the leadership as to the ultimate outcome.

314

1923

314. The Minister for Home Affairs, Kevin O'Higgins addresses newly matriculated Civic Guards in a fiery speech. Seeing this interesting actuality photograph one can perhaps be persuaded that the account given in the Dail Debates of O'Higgins's venemous attack on Erskine Childers before his execution, is not out of character. The hatred which he showed towards de Valera must also be taken into account as a factor prolonging the fighting. Intransigence and inflexibility were not a monopoly of either side in the Civil War and these characteristics were to impede progress towards peace. The mass executions by land mines carried out in Ballyseedy, County Kerry, by troops under General Daly, and the deliberate entombment of Republican fighters in the mines on Mount Gabriel were not only to lose him his command, but were also to embitter relationships between the opposing sides, making peace negotiations harder to reach.

315

315. Delegates of the Neutral IRA entering the Scala Theatre, Dublin for their convention. From the very beginning of the Civil War there were IRA men who, although they had served loyally in the Tan War, had come to the decision that they could take no part on either side in Civil War. Early in 1923 they formed an association and held a large convention at the Scala Theatre in Dublin at which an appeal for a truce of one month was drafted and sent to President de Valera, to General Mulcahy, to Commandant Liam Lynch and to President Cosgrave. Published in the newspapers on Saturday, 17 February 1923, it was rejected by all but de Valera, and another moment when the war might have been ended passed.

316

317

316. Through reports that he received from other commanders, Liam Lynch, Chief of Staff of the IRA, became aware that some of them now held the opinion that the IRA would no longer be in a position to sustain a campaign throughout the long bright days of the summer of 1923. In spite of the very grave risks involved, it was decided to summon a meeting of the Army Executive and to invite President de Valera to attend. Evading recognition and capture with enormous difficulty, ten of the Executive and de Valera met in a small cottage in the remote Nier Valley, between the Comeragh and the Monavullagh Mountains south of Clonmell on 24 March. At the end of this meeting a vote was taken and the proposal to bring the war to an end was lost by one vote. However, it was decided to postpone the decision until all of the members of the Executive could be present and de Valera received a mandate to have a proposal for a peace settlement ready. The commanders and de Valera dispersed. But word of this concentration of Republican leaders reached Mulcahy and Prout and one of the biggest concentrations of troops yet assembled was mounted to surround them. Liam Lynch, while leading a small party in an attempt to escape to the south across the Knockmealdowns, was shot at long range. He was carried onwards by Frank Aiken, Sean Hyde and Bill Quirk, until finding that they were unable to move fast enough with their burden, he ordered them to leave him lying in the heather. He was soon captured and carried, agonizingly, down to Newcastle on an improvised stretcher. General Prout himself came to meet him there, bringing an ambulance so that Lynch might have every care, but he died that night, 10 April.

317. Commandant Dan Breen TD, was one of the last of the surviving leaders of the IRA to be captured on 14 April 1923. Although it did not declare for peace, the meeting of the IRA in the Nier Valley was instrumental in bringing peace nearer as it resulted in the capture of so many of the upper echelon of the IRA. Its already greatly weakened potential for hostilities was further diminished. After escaping Prout's drag-net and spending nights on the mountains drinking melted snow, Breen eventually got to a dug-out in the Glen of Aherlow where he was captured the following morning. By this time, the majority of those of the Executive still at liberty had become convinced that a cease-fire must take place. The postponed meeting took place on 20 April, at Poulacapple, near Mullinahone, County Tipperary and the decision was made to empower de Valera to open negotiations for a peace settlement.

318. Free State soldiers searching a train for Republicans, April 1923. Neither the Free State side nor the Republicans reached an agreement, but, after a cease-fire called by the Chief-of-Staff, General Frank Aiken, for 30 April, and an order from him to dump arms given on 24 May, together with an address from Eamon de Valera as President of Sinn Fein and leader of the shadow civil administration, the Irish Civil War was brought to a close on that date. The defeat of the Republicans had been achieved, as the Commander-in-Chief of the British Army in Ireland expressed it '...by means far more drastic than any which the British Government dared to impose during the worst period of the Rebellion'. The British Lord Chancellor, Lord Birkenhead, (F.E. Smith) said that a united Irish Volunteer Force cound not have been defeated with less than 200,000 troops and concluded 'Parliament would not have granted you the money and the country would not have given you the Volunteers.' Indeed, with the unstable conditions prevailing in England in 1922–3, Lloyd George's 'immediate and terrible war' could have provoked a social revolution there. At the time of the cessation of hostilities, there were 11,316 war prisoners in Irish camps and prisons, two hundred of whom were women.

319. Women reading Free State election posters at Ennis, County Clare, August 1923. Only Cosgrave's party election posters are visible, and those of the Labour Party had been posted over. When the war ended, emergency legislation was enacted to give a legal framework for continuing to hold prisoners in gaol until after the snap election the government had decided to call in August. De Valera had been nominated for his old seat in East Clare and was determined to get to Ennis to address his constituents.

318

319

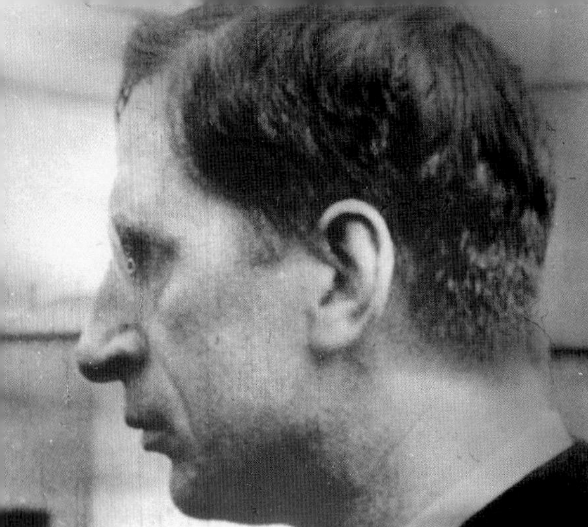

320

320. De Valera speaking to the crowd at Ennis, County Clare, 15 August 1923. He had only just stood up and begun to speak when a company of Free State soldiers drawn up in the square and supported by a 'Whippet', started firing their rifles into the air and advancing on the platform. This caused panic in the crowd as several people were hit by pellets from the rifles which had been loaded with bird shot. There was confusion on the platform during which de Valera was knocked down, but on regaining his feet he saw that the soldiers were preparing to fire a second volley. The troops surrounded the platform and de Valera descending from it, gave himself up to avoid any further woundings.

321. Some of the crowd running from the shooting at the Ennis election meeting. De Valera was led away under military escort and imprisoned in Arbour Hill Prison, Dublin, then later transferred to Kilmainham Gaol where he was held without any charge being preferred against him for nearly a year. When the votes were counted de Valera was seen to have headed the poll but, like all the other Sinn Fein candidates, he intended to refuse the oath of allegiance to the British king.

321

322

322. Free State soldiers remove furniture in a raid on the Sinn Fein Party headquarters in Suffolk Street, Dublin. Alarmed at the support that Sinn Fein was receiving, Kevin O'Higgins as Minister for Home Affairs made every effort to seize election literature and posters, disorganize canvassing by arbitrary arrests and, on Saturday 18 August, the headquarters of the Sinn Fein Party was raided and their director of elections imprisoned without charge.

323. William T. Cosgrave, President of the Executive Committee of the Irish Free State. With 63 of his party in the assembly and the 44 members of the Sinn Fein party returned in the general election debarred from taking their seats by the oath of allegiance, and opposed by a Labour Party having only 14 seats, the Cosgrave regime seemed firmly in the saddle. He had no difficulty in passing a Public Safety Act on 2 July 1923 that allowed him to continue to arrest and hold prisoners without bringing charges against them in the courts; similar acts were to be a continuing feature of Cosgrave's administration.

323

324

1923

324. General Richard Mulcahy, Minister for Defence (*left*) with Mr Ernest Blythe, Minister for Finance. General Mulcahy retained his portfolio in the 1923 Executive Council, while Ernest Blythe was given that of Finance. The IRB was still active, having supported Collins in the Treaty Campaign. A number of Free State Army officers with IRB affiliations now formed an association which called itself 'the Old IRA'. Mulcahy vehemently opposed this organization and set up another, rival one. The split in the Free State Army became so serious that General Mulcahy was obliged to resign. The 'Old IRA' still exists today as a much respected veterans association. Ernest Blythe, in charge of finance, began to reveal the financial stings in the tail of the Treaty, notably the Land Annuity payments that had to be made to the British government and other financial obligations.

325. President Cosgrave went to Geneva to make a formal application for the Irish Free State's membership of the League of Nations, which was granted on 10 September 1923. Here he is seen on the bridge of the British and Irish Steam Packet vessel *SS Lady Louth*, with the captain, just passing the Poolbeg lighthouse at the entrance to the Liffey on his return from Geneva.

326

1924 326. Mary MacSwiney on hunger-strike outside Mountjoy Prison, Dublin. Five months after the end of the Civil War, many hundreds of prisoners remained in gaols and camps without any charges being made against them and in October a move was made to reduce their status and treatment to that of criminals. As had always happened in the past, 424 prisoners went on hunger-strike in Mountjoy Prison. The women of Cuman na m'Bán established a picket outside the gates, where Mary MacSwiney, sister of Terence MacSwiney, went on a sympathetic hunger-strike. She is seen here (*second from the right*) with a blanket over her knees; on her right is the tall figure of Madame Maude Gonne MacBride and on her left is that grand old lady of Irish and English left-wing politics, Mrs Charlotte Despard, sister of the Earl of Ypres. Throughout her long life she was progressive and anti-colonialist in outlook. By years of persistent effort she had been instrumental in improving the lot of the London poor and had been a leading light in the achievement of votes for women. Now, in her late seventies, she continued to support the cause of human rights. The bravery, tenacity and dignity of this wonderful woman and her achievements remain her lasting monument.

327. Grace Plunkett *née* Gifford, staunch Republican and the artist wife of Joseph Plunkett, spent many long months in Kilmainham Gaol. This is a little mural that she painted on the wall of her gloomy cell a little before her release in May 1924.

327

328

328. The Labour leader Cathal O'Shannon (*on the extreme right*) at Wolfe Tone's grave, Bodenstown, 21 June 1924. The Irish Labour Party, founded by James Connolly, formed, in the years immediately after the Civil War the only unified and consistent opposition in the Dail to the Cosgrave regime and its voice was constantly raised against the repeated infringements of personal liberty that continued to be a feature of that administration, as well as making reiterated pleas for the release of the prisoners.

329. The Boundary Commission, seen here at one of its inaugural meetings in 1924, with Eoin MacNeill on the extreme right. Its ineffectuality showed how unrealistic were Michael Collins' hopes that it would be able to obtain gains for the Free State which would result in a transfer of Catholics and Nationalists in the north of Ireland into the Free State jurisdiction. Making use of their unassailable position, the Northern government refused to countenance any significant changes and the Boundary Commission foundered.

329

330

1924–25

330. Mrs Charlotte Despard (*left*) and Madame Maude Gonne MacBride at Mountjoy Gaol, await the delivery of the bodies of Rory O'Connor and other executed Republicans in November 1924. As well as the bodies of the executed, living prisoners now began to be released from the prisons and camps in greater numbers.

331

331. De Valera (*centre figure*) at the Sinn Fein convention of 20 November 1925 along with his supporters: on de Valera's right is George Daly, General Secretary of Sinn Fein, and on his immediate left is Miss Barton, sister of one of the signatories of the Treaty Agreement, and on her left is Countess Markievicz. On the extreme right of the photograph is Eamon Donnelly, Sinn Fein Director of Elections. The constant domination of Sinn Fein by the IRA Executive made de Valera's task of forming a credible alternative civil administration increasingly difficult. A number of leading members close to him in their views, began to press for change. The Free State administration was growing stronger every day while the Republican position was being eroded. This split in Sinn Fein widened still further at the IRA convention of 17 November 1925, when a motion tabled by Peadar O'Donnell, proposing that the still very tenuous element of civilian control of the IRA exercised by Sinn Fein should be abolished, was passed by a large majority. At the Sinn Fein convention held a few days later, de Valera and his supporters took a firm stand against this.

332. President Cosgrave assisting at the raising, on 13 August 1925, of the first pylon in the grid system that would supply electricity from a huge generator at Arnacrusha on the River Shannon near Limerick. Amid the social unrest and distress of the first years of the Free State, the Cosgrave administration was responsible for a notable and lasting achievement – the inauguration of the 'Shannon Scheme'. This ambitious development had been too large and costly to tempt any private capital in Ireland to invest in it, so in a move quite unusual at this time, it was built with public funding. It is not too much to say that this scheme was an important factor in aiding the economic recovery from the disaster of Civil War, both in the immediate employment it offered and in the subsequent availability of cheaper electric power throughout the Free State. It is still in operation today.

332

333

333. The founding members of the Fianna Fail Party on the day of its establishment, 16 May 1926: (*from right to left*) Domhnall O'Buachalla (*only half in picture*), who was later to be the last Governor General of the Irish Free State; Mrs Tom Clarke; de Valera; and Constance Markievicz, who had less than a year to live. Four months after the November meeting of Sinn Fein, another meeting was called at which the proposals to enter constitutional politics were rejected and President de Valera and his supporters resigned from the Sinn Fein Party. They proceeded at once to set about the foundation of a new party that was to pursue Republican aims by constitutional means. The Fianna Fail party was the result.

334

334. The leading members of the Labour Party. President Cosgrave called a general election in June 1927. Unexpectedly his party's seats were reduced to 47 while Fianna Fail won 44 and Labour 22. With the cooperation of smaller parties and independents it seemed possible that the government might be overturned if Fianna Fail deputies could take their seats.

335. Thomas Johnson, leader of the Labour Party which had formed virtually the only opposition in the Dail to Cosgrave's policies, although its numbers had always been too few to influence legislation. Now, in Johnson's view, there appeared to be the possibility of forming a coalition with Fianna Fail and a number of independents in order to overturn the government.

335

336

336. De Valera leads the elected Fianna Fail members into Leinster House on 23 June 1927. On the opening day of the new parliamentary session, de Valera made a formal attempt to secure his party in their seats without taking the oath of allegiance.

337

337. Newspaper photographers and reporters cluster around the doorway of the Dail to know the result of de Valera's initiative. His legal advisers had told him that the oath could not be enforced before the Speaker of the House had been elected and that, in the meantime they could vote for whoever they wished as Speaker. But they were told that this would not be accepted and that they must take the oath first. A few weeks later the Minister for Home Affairs, Kevin O'Higgins, was shot dead by two IRA men acting without the authority from the Army Executive. This produced such a grave political crisis that de Valera decided that the Fianna Fail deputies must secure entry into the Chamber and on 11 July, he led them once again into Leinster House and, on behalf of the Fianna Fail Parliamentary Party, he declared to the Clerk of the Dail that he was not taking any oath and signed the book presented to him by Colm Ó Murchadha. The other Fianna Fail deputies followed suit and, taking their places in the Chamber, brought a fundamental change to the Irish political scene. On 16 August, Thomas Johnson moved a vote of no confidence in the government and but for the absence of one National League Party member, John Jinks, of Sligo, the government would have fallen.

338

338. Following the death of Timothy Healy in January 1928, James MacNeill (*above*), brother of the co-founder of the Gaelic League, Eoin MacNeill, was installed as the second Governor General of the Irish Free State. James MacNeill had previously served as High Commissioner for the Irish Free State in London.

339. President Cosgrave opened the rebuilt General Post Office in April 1928 on the thirteenth anniversary of the Easter Rising, but this celebration of freedom was not to be without its ironies. In 1925 a bill, opposed by Labour, and the poet Yeats as a senator, had been passed by the Cosgrave regime totally prohibiting divorce in the Free State. Another bill had just been passed, as though to contradict the notion of freedom created by the GPO ceremony, making all books and papers subject to censorship and appointing a permanent board for that purpose, the notorious Censorship of Publications Board. In the course of the years it committed so many gaffes by banning our most distinguished writers that it was, at length, laughed more and more into the shadows where it still subsists today, having over the years, learned from unhappy experience, to act with extreme caution. This year was also remarkable for two very singular events: the first was a bill totally prohibiting artificial contraception; the second, that in order to vote in favour of the Censorship of Publications Bill, Sir James Craig journeyed to Dublin, took his seat in the Dail as a member for Trinity College and gave the first example of cross-border cooperation in repressive legislation!

339

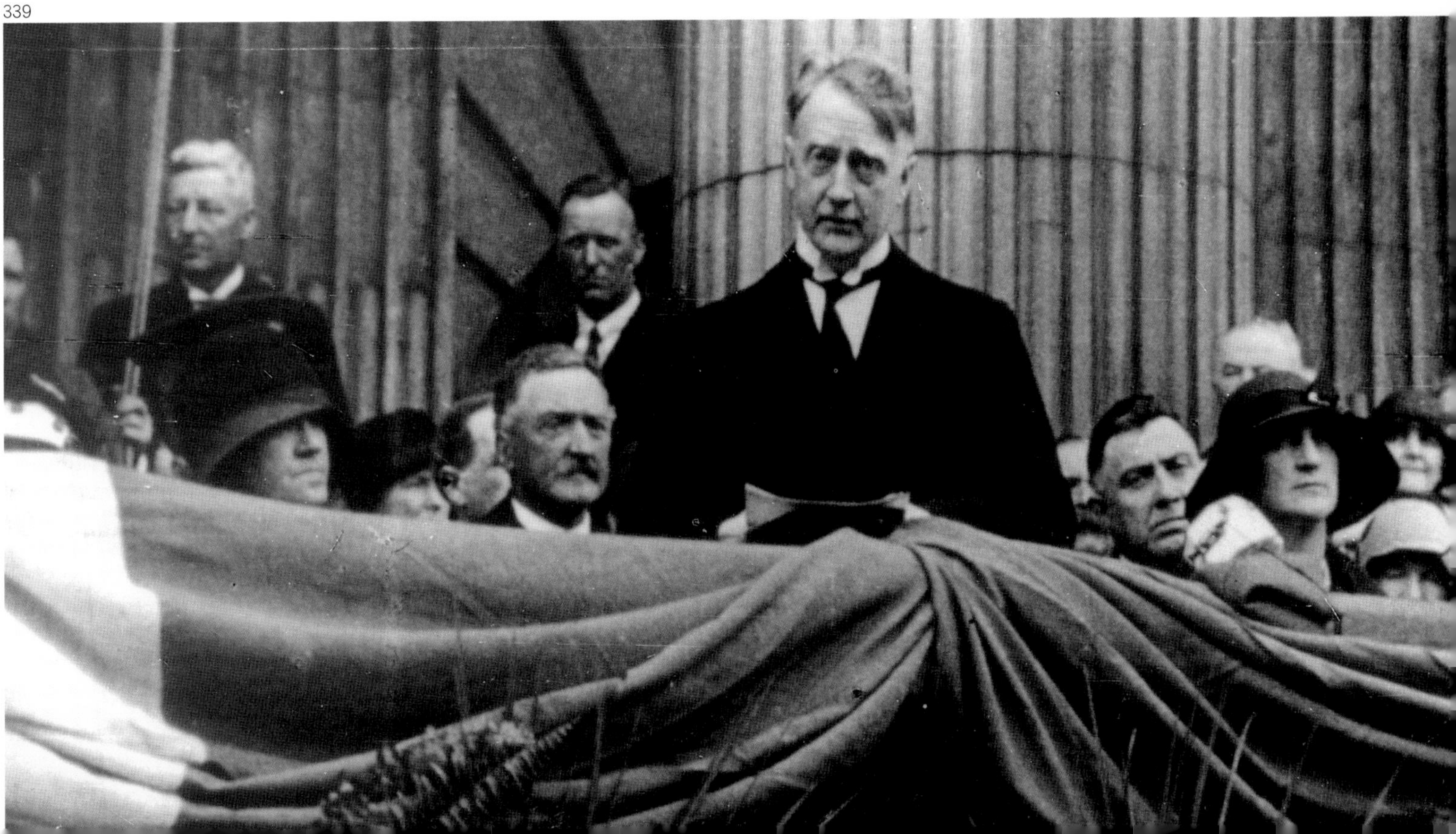

340

1928

340. Stormont, the Parliament Building in Belfast. This fine imposing building, superbly set in rolling grassland diversified by trees, became the seat of government in Northern Ireland for almost fifty years. Throughout that time power remained so firmly in the hands of the Ulster Unionist Party that Northern Ireland was, virtually, a one-party state. Sir Edward Carson was elevated to the peerage as Baron Glencairn and had become a Lord of Appeal at Westminster, while the prime minister, Sir James Craig, became Lord Craigavon. This Imperial-style building remains; the Empire has gone.

341

342

341. De Valera speaking at Ennis, County Clare in the run-up to the general election of 1932. A continually increasing swing away from Cosgrave's party and to Fianna Fail was now taking place. The Republican vote, paralyzed by internment and the enforcement of the oath had remained dormant for some years, but with Republican deputies in the Dail and Fianna Fail making the release of internees a plank in their platform, the vote was beginning to swing their way.

342. De Valera's party did not get an overall majority in 1932, but enough to be able to form a government with the support of the Labour Party and some independents. It was not a sufficiently secure basis to enable him to put through all his policies and he took the brave step of going to the country again in three months' time in 1933. This time Fianna Fail was returned with a substantial overall majority.

343. Domhnall Ó Buachalla reads the letter from de Valera appointing him as Governor General of the Irish Free State, November 1932. De Valera had learned many bitter lessons in *real politik* before and during the Civil War and now approached the solution of constitutional problems with increased flexibility. He was determined gradually to eliminate all vestiges of the former Imperial power from the political structure of the country and the presence, demanded by the constitution of the Irish Free State, of a Governor General residing, as James MacNeill did, in the Vice-Regal Lodge, was an early target. But how to reduce the status of this office? De Valera had thought of a very clever way. He selected from among the staunchest of his Republican supporters a colleague whom he knew to be steadfast and incorruptible, and nominated him. This man, living in a modest suburban house, agreed to continue living there and never to take part in any public event or ceremony, but merely to sign any State documents when necessary. For a time, the Vice-Regal Lodge remained empty. The representative of the king had become a ghostly presence. This move was the first public expression of de Valera's new way in politics.

344

1932

343

344. The release of the first 25 Republican internees on 10 March 1932 brought a large section of the population behind de Valera, and it was just as well that it did so for things were taking a very peculiar turn on the other side of the political divide.

345

1933

345. Mr and Mrs Cosgrave after casting their votes in 1933. The administration that had won the Civil War had lost the Civil Peace. The power structure that had used ever more tyrannical means to cling to power had crumbled. The most astonishing and even absurd accusations were launched at de Valera at this time; accusations that seem comical in their absurdity to us today, such as, for example, that he was a communist!

346

346. Fianna Fail election posters from 1933. Even while the 1933 general election was taking place, moves were afoot behind the scenes. Being fairly sure that it was in for a political defeat, the far right was assembling its forces for a new effort to regain control by setting up a political structure not before seen in Southern Ireland.

347. President De Valera and his Executive Council, 1933. One of the most important planks in the Fianna Fail electoral platform had been the abolition of the Land Annuity payments, a financial burden imposed by the Treaty. This led to the imposition of extra duties on Irish goods by Westminster, a situation called the 'Economic War' which lasted until 1938 and brought great hardship to the smaller farmers. But a more immediate and dangerous threat was about to appear.

347

1934

348. The Blueshirts give the Fascist Salute as they parade at Bluebell Cemetery, Dublin, 1934. A group of veterans of the Free State Army, formed a few years previously and known as the Army Comrades Association, was increasingly unhappy at the gradual restoration to power of many of those whom they had fought, and as they thought, subdued. With the encouragement of Ernest Blythe, Professor Tierney of University College Dublin and the more right-wing elements in the Association, General O'Duffy, former Commissioner for Police under the Cosgrave administration, was elected to the leadership of the Army Comrades Association in July 1933. He immediately changed its name to 'the National Guard', opened its membership to the public, but with a religious test, and instituted the wearing of a uniform. Shortly after this he announced that the membership exceeded 30,000 and that there would be a nationwide march of 20,000 members to Leinster Lawn, in front of the Dail. De Valera and the Executive Council feared a Fascist style putsh , not unreasonably, as some of their leaders, such as Captain Quish of Limerick, had said 'The Government are a crowd of Spaniards, Jews and Manxmen. If necessary we will use the guns again to redeem the people.' They finally became known as the Blueshirts. De Valera was reluctantly obliged to make use of the Special Powers that the Cosgrave administration had put in place. O'Duffy had sought the support of the Catholic hierarchy, assuming that the Irish Church would give its backing in the same way that the hierarchies of Italy and Portugal had done and that the Spanish would do, but he received a fatal rebuff. The Irish hierarchy would do nothing of the kind. This decision helped to save Ireland from what would have been nothing short of a disaster. The movement dwindled away, the last of them, led by O'Duffy, went off to Spain, 700 strong, to fight for Franco and, it is said, made military history by returning as 701! After this, Ernest Blythe retired from public life to become director and subsequently chief share-holder of the Abbey Theatre and Dr Tierney became Chancellor of the National University of Ireland.

348

350

1938–40

349. President de Valera and Dr Frank Ryan, Minister of Agriculture (*in the background*) arrive in London on 16 January 1938. A new constitution came into force on 29 December 1937, removing permanently the Governor General and substituting an elected President, who was soon to be Dr Douglas Hyde, founder of the Gaelic League. Aspects of that constitution, particularly with regard to the status of women and the right to divorce are as controversial today as they were then, but it paved the way for the next step, a further advance towards Irish sovereignty. De Valera indicated to the British premier, Neville Chamberlain and his cabinet that as war was now inevitable, it would be much easier to supply Britain with food if what had been the Irish Free State was allowed to become a neutral country, for which he proposed the name of Éire, but to do this would require the withdrawal of the remaining British soldiers garrisoning three posts. Of course the 'Economic War' would have to go too. He was successful in all his endeavors and returned to Ireland to make preparations for a coming general election.

350. De Valera addressing a large crowd outside the Bank of Ireland, College Green, Dublin, during the run-up to the general election of June 1938. This election returned the Fianna Fail party with a powerful majority of 77 seats at a time when unequivocal political unity was to be greatly needed; World War II was on its way.

349

351

351. The Éire Customs hut at Carrickarnon on the border with Northern Ireland, December 1939. Éire came into being as a neutral country, yet its neutrality subtly favoured the Allies. There were controversial moments, such as when an American ambassador expressed a view that Éire should be occupied, but these passed under the able statesmanship of de Valera. However, even World War II, referred to at the time by that truly remarkable Irish euphemism 'the Emergency', had failed to bring together, on one platform, the representatives of the two parties which had opposed one another since the Civil War. Throughout the whole time of what has become known as the 'phoney war' this dichotomy continued. It was the sweep of the German armies across Holland, Belgium and France that was to shock the members of both parties into a radical adjustment of their relationship.

352, 353. The two parties met on one platform, together with the representatives of the Labour Party, before a huge gathering (*see overleaf, 353*) in College Green, Dublin, at the identical spot where Michael Collins had opened his pro-Treaty campaign only eighteen years before. It was one of the most memorable events in the modern history of Ireland, for a great conflict had been instrumental in healing the aftermath of a small one. The future relationships of the parties from that point on would never be the same.

352

The antagonistic tension that convulsed what is now the Irish Republic and has been the subject of this book is, regrettably, still present in Northern Ireland where the majority community has always shown a sense of political insecurity without powerful support from what used to be the Empire, and as that successor to the Empire, the Commonwealth, itself undergoes the changes imposed by evolution, a habit of referring to England as 'the mainland' has come into use. There is, indeed, a mainland. On a clear day, from the pale grey cliffs of Dover can be seen the pale gray Cap Gris-Nez, that prominence on the coast of the great continent of Afroeurasia, the world's largest land mass. Hereabouts we are all islanders, even as we are all islanders on Planet Earth.

1940

353

A Note on the Photographs

Although excellent miniature cameras were available in 1922, the film emulsions available in Ireland at the time did not have a fine enough grain structure to allow their use for press purposes. As a result, almost all photographs were taken on quite large glass plates, with cameras such as the Speed Graphic or Ensign. The plates were heavy, fragile and slow to change, hence no follow-through-on-action shots, as we know them today, exist from still photographic sources of the time.

Many of the photographs are of subjects only covered by amateur photographers using film. To get the best results from these, it has been necessary in some cases to remove the photographic emulsion from its celluloid base and mount it between glass plates in a medium of the same refractive index, a process that removes the effects of surface scratching and also greatly reduces reflective scattering, enabling an optimization of the image to be submitted for final electronic enhancement. This procedure is especially necessary where very fine detail is needed.

A word about the photographers and their styles is necessary. Unquestionably the most advanced of the still photographers was Joseph Cashman, both in respect of subject choice and *cadrage*; the Keogh brothers, while making some good portrait studies, were much less adroit at discovering original set-ups, although the slower emulsions which the latter used and their small working stops enable far better extraction of detail from their higher definition images. Among the cinematographers, Gordon Lewis stands out pre-eminently, particularly when he began using his new camera, a Precynsky's Aeroscope, in December 1921, with its much improved motion-picture lens. All the motion-picture frames were submitted to the regime referred to earlier which enables an improved quality to be achieved from a far from ideal source, although the motion-picture sources are far more satisfactory in providing better and more spontaneous close shots than do most still photographs of the period.

We know that a number of the photographs were intended and were carefully taken for propaganda purposes, both by the British and the Free State, and this is commented on in the text of the captions. The Sinn Fein Party's Director of Publicity, Desmond FitzGerald, father of a future prime minister, was one of Ireland's earliest media men with a real appreciation of the importance of photography in communications. Alas, this was not the case with his opposite number on the Republican side, Erskine Childers, so that we have very little visual material from this side of the struggle. It is to Mrs Childers that we owe the fine coverage of the voyage of the *Asgard*.

An amusing detail seen in many of the photographs was the fact that the great majority of people in 1922 were still freezing into immobility at the sight of a camera, although the need for this had disappeared thirty years previously, as can be seen from the wonderful photographs of Count Primoli in the 1890s. Even today one observes this reaction occasionally.

Endnotes

1 Winston S. Churchill, *Lord Randolph Churchill*, 2 vols, Odhams, 1906, vol. II, p.59.
2 Ibid.
3 The Weekly Summary, Dublin Castle, 27/8/20.
4 For these quotations and an account of British Cabinet policy towards Partition, see Chapter 13, 'Setting Up the Six', in *Michael Collins* by Tim Pat Coogan, Hutchinson, London, 1990.
5 CAB 23/83, PRO, London.
6 Several of Collins' contemporaries have testified to his bewilderment and anger at de Valera's proposal. The long whore quotation is taken from Frank O'Connor's book, *The Big Fellow*, Corgi, 1960.
7 The correspondence which was subsequently published in pamphlet form is available in a number of archives, including the PRO, London; The National Library, Dublin; and the National Archives, Dublin.
8 Robert Barton, 'Notes for a Lecture', PRO, Dublin, MS 1093/14.
9 Michael Collins, in Treaty Debates, Dail Reports, SO, p.32.
10 P.S. Hegarty, *The Victory of Sinn Fein*, Talbot Press, 1924, pps. 86–7.
11 Mrs Tom Clarke, Private Sessions, Dail Éireann, 17/12/21. p.262.
12 Ironically, it was de Valera who first referred publicly, in the Dail, to the plan which Collins had drawn up, containing this remark, for a ruthless onslaught should the truce fail, 26/8/21. See also Private Sessions, Dail Eireann, 1921–22, SO, p.77.
13 O'Hegarty, op cit.
14 De Valera to McGarrity, quoted in *The McGarrity Papers*, by Sean Cronin, Anvil, 1972, pps. 109–11. McGarrity was the principal Irish-American leader to support de Valera during his American stay, but he later split from de Valera, charging him with abandoning the Republican ideal.
15 Quoted by T.P. Coogan in *Michael Collins*, Hutchinson, London, 1990, p.231.
16 Coogan, op. cit., p.251.
17 Leon O'Broin, *Michael Collins*, Gill & Macmillan, 1980, p.103.
18 Coogan, op. cit., pps.256–7.
19 Collins, in fact, said in the course of the Treaty debates: 'In my opinion it [The Treaty] gives us freedom, not the ultimate freedom that all nations aspire and develop to, but the freedom to achieve it...'
20 Coogan, op. cit., p.276.
21 There are extensive references to the O'Mara interlude in the O'Mara papers. National Library of Ireland, MS. 21, 549 (2). In particular, an unpublished MS by an O'Mara daughter, Patricia Lavelle, which she read to de Valera. The subsequent, somewhat altered volume was published as *James O'Mara*, by Patricia Lavelle, Clonmore and Reynolds, 1961. See also *De Valera, Long Fellow, Long Shadow*, by T.P. Coogan, Hutchinson, London, and *Michael Collins*, New York, Chapter 5.
22 Quoted by Coogan, op. cit.
23 This account of de Valera's statements and actions after learning of the Treaty's signing can be studied in either Coogan's biographies of Collins and de Valera or a number of other works mentioned in the biographies of these works.
24 Erskine Childers Diary, 9/12/21. Trinity College Dublin, Manuscript Library.
25 Coogan, *Michael Collins*, p.299.
26 Ibid.
27 Ibid.
28 Letter in the author's possession, dated 1/2/88 from Joseph Honan, a son of de Valera's principal Clare election worker, who was present during the incident described.
29 Quoted by Michael Hopkinson, *Green Against Green*, Gill & Macmillan, 1988.
30 This O'Higgins address, delivered in 1924, is quoted by a number of authors on the period, c/f. Michael Hopkinson, *Green Against Green*, Gill & Macmillan, 1988, p.53.
31 The extract is taken from one of a series of letters O'Malley wrote to Molly Childers, Erskine Childers' widow, which are deposited in Trinity College Dublin. Quoted by Hopkinson, *Green Against Green*, p.270.
32 Quoted by T.P. Coogan, *Eamon de Valera*, Hutchinson, 1993.
33 Longford and O'Neill, *Eamon de Valera*, Hutchinson, London, 1970.
34 De Valera to Edith Ellis, 26/2/23, Mulcahy pps., University College Dublin Archive, p.7/B/89.
35 *Irish Independent*, March 23, 1922.
36 Senator Farrell, Seanad Reports, Senate 20, 1876, quoted Donal O'Sullivan, Irish Free State and its Senate, Faber, 1910, p.19.
37 Ernie O'Malley, *The Singing Flame*, Anvil, 1978.
38 Craig was addressing a group of Belfast businessmen on 3/4/22. Quoted in Coogan, *Michael Collins*, p. 348.
39 Churchill's remarks and those of Lloyd George and Lionel Curtiss are described in CAB 21/49, PRO. London.
40 Hansard 26/6, 22.
41 From the poem 'Remorse for Intemperate Speech' by W.B. Yeats, Gill & Macmillan, 1989, A. Norman Jeffares, ed.
42 Blythe papers, UCD, p.24/554.
43 These committee reports are contained in the Irish National Archives, boxes S 10111 and S 11195.
44 Ricardo to Tallents, CO 906/27, PRO, London.
45 Quoted in Coogan, *Michael Collins*, p.352.
46 Copy in author's possession.
47 Original in Irish National Archives, quoted in Coogan, *Michael Collins*, p.358.
48 Churchill in House of Commons, 26/6.22, Hansard.
49 CO 906/30, PRO London.
50 CO 739/16, PRO, London.
51 Quoted in Coogan, *Michael Collins*, p.367.
52 Craig to Lloyd George, 8/2/22. CAB 21/254. PRO, London.
53 Hales made the comment to Eamonn de Barra, a Cork Republican, on 29 December 1921, when the Treaty debate was in progress. The author subsequently conducted a number of interviews with de Barra.
54 O'Malley notebooks, UCD, p.17b/193.
55 Report by Seamus Woods, OC, 3rd. Northern Division, Mulcahy pps., UCD.
56 Quoted by Coogan, *Michael Collins*, p.396.
57 Ibid.
58 Ibid, 411.
59 Quoted in Coogan, pps. 396–8.
60 PG. 94, 19/8/2.
61 Quoted by Hopkinson, *Green Against Green*, p.143.
62 Ibid.
63 Ibid, p.148.
64. Ibid.
65 The creation of this 'government' is described in Coogan, *de Valera*, pps. 338–9.
66 Valiulis, Maryann, *General Richard Mulcahy*, Irish Academic Press, 1992, pps.175–6.
67 Dail Debataxs, No.17, 1922.
68 Mulcahy ps, UCD, quoted by Coogan, *Michael Collins*, p.205.
69 Copy in author's possession.
70. Quoted in Longford, O'Neill, *de Valera*, p.213.
71 *Irish Independent*, 10.3.1923.
72 O'Donoghue was a founder of the Irish Bureau of Military History. His papers are in the National Library of Ireland.
73 Quoted by Hopkinson, p.234.
74 Quoted in Coogan, *de Valera*, p.354. The account of the ending of the Civil War is based on several sources including the author's own cited works, de Valera's official biography by Longford and O'Neill and works by Dorothy Macardle, Mary Bromage and Maryann Valiulis.
75 Ibid.

Select Bibliography

Coogan, Tim Pat, *Michael Collins*, Hutchinson, London, 1990.
Coogan, Tim Pat, *Long Fellow, Long Shadow*, Hutchinson, London, 1993.
Longford, Lord, and O'Neil, T.P., *Eamon de Valera*, Hutchinson, London, 1970.
Bromage, Mary C., *De Valera and the March of a Nation*, Hutchinson, London, 1956.
Hopkinson, Michael, *Green Against Green*, Gill & Macmillan, Dublin, 1988.
Macardle, Dorothy, *The Irish Republic*, Irish Press, Dublin, 1951.
Valiulis, Maryann, *General Richard Mulcahy, Portrait of a Revolutionary*, Irish Academic Press, Dublin, 1992.

Index

Published by
ROBERTS RINEHART PUBLISHERS
6309 Monarch Park Place
Niwot, Colorado 80503
TEL 303.652.2685
FAX 303.652.2689
www.robertsrinehart.com

Distributed to the trade by Publishers Group West

First published in 1998 by
Weidenfeld & Nicolson
Orion Publishing Group
5 Upper St Martin's Lane
London WC2H 9EA

ISBN 1-57098-252-X

Library of Congress Catalog Card Number 98-87783

All rights reserved. No part of this publication may be copied, reproduced or transmitted in any form or by any means, without permission of the publishers.

Text copyright The Irish Civil War Its Origins and Course © Tim Pat Coogan; The Pictorial Record © George Morrison
Design and layout copyright © Weidenfeld & Nicolson 1998

Art Direction by David Rowley
Designed by Mark Vernon-Jones
Edited by Marilyn Inglis

Printed in Italy

10 9 8 7 6 5 4 3 2 1

Photo credits

All photographs in this book are the copyright of George Morrison except those belonging to the Cashman Collection which appear on pages 2, 3; and those belonging to the Hulton-Getty Library on the front and back cover and pages 12, 13, 14, 15, 16, 17, 18, 19, 29, 32, 46, 47, 48 and 49 within Tim Pat Coogan's chapter entitled *The Irish Civil War – Its Origins and Course*. Those which appear in *The Pictorial Record* (listed here by picture number) are also the copyright of George Morrision, with the exception of pictures 2,13, 20, 26, 61, 90, 100, 105, 112, 120, 123, 130, 131, 132, 139, 140, 151, 152, 156, 157, 158, 162, 172, 173, 179, 188, 193, 195, 207, 208, 210, 216, 219, 220, 225, 229, 231, 232, 234 which are the copyright of the Hulton-Getty Library and pictures 30, 140, 189, 196, 197, 214, 236, 287 which are the copyright of the Cashman Collection.

9967065